Dive Bomber

Dive Bomber

LEARNING TO FLY THE NAVY'S FIGHTING PLANES

Robert A. Winston

Illustrated by Walter I. Dothard

Naval Institute Press
Annapolis, Maryland

This is a facsimile edition of the book originally published in 1939 by Holiday House, Inc.

Library of Congress Cataloging-in-Publication Data

Winston, Robert A. (Robert Alexander), 1907–
    Dive bomber : learning to fly the Navy's fighting planes / Robert A. Winston ; illustrated by Walter I. Dothard.
      p. cm.
    Reprint. Originally published: New York : Holiday House, 1939.
    ISBN 1-55750-901-8
    1. United States.   Navy—Aviation.   2. Aeronautics, Military—
—United States.   3. Dive bombers.   I. Title.
VG93.W513   1991
359.9'4834'0973—dc20   90-22874

Printed in the United States of America on acid-free paper ⊗

9 8 7 6 5 4 3 2

First printing

Foreword

THE opinions and assertions contained herein are the private ones of the writer and are not to be construed as official or reflecting the views of the Navy Department or the naval service at large.

Some of the material in these pages is reprinted through the courtesy of the *Sportsman Pilot, Popular Aviation, Ken,* and the *Reader's Digest,* whose kind permission is gratefully acknowledged.

Especial credit is due Mr. Walter I. Dothard, Sr., whose careful and accurate illustrations of the various types of service airplanes are an integral and essential part of this book, and to his son, Ensign Walter I. Dothard, Jr., U.S.N.R., my former shipmate and fellow instructor, who did much of the research in connection with the illustrations.

R. A. WINSTON, Lieutenant, U. S. N.
Bureau of Aeronautics,
Navy Department,
Washington, D. C.

November 11, 1941

Contents

List of Illustrations

Dive Bomber

CHAPTER ONE

Off the Deep End

EIGHTEEN DOLLARS AN HOUR. THAT WAS WHAT they wanted for dual instruction at the flying school on Long Island. I had expected flying lessons to be expensive, but I didn't think they were going to tear such a hole in my pay-check.

"Haven't you anything a little lower?" I asked hopefully.

"Not in our school," was the short answer. "Of course if you just want to play around the airport in light planes, some of these private operators will take your money, but you won't learn much flying."

"I'll think it over," I said.

As I walked away from the hangar, my hopes sank. Flying was a rich man's game, I decided. Even a private flying license would eat up about two month's salary, and a commercial license would cost a young fortune. I'd have to wait until the depression was over, at least.

If I had waited for that, I'd be waiting yet. But fortunately, a friend of mine who worked with me ran across a newspaper article.

"If you're interested in flying," he said, "why don't you try the Navy? It says here that they're taking on men right and left."

"The Navy?" I repeated. "Who wants to fly seaplanes around all the time?"

"They have landplanes too, on the aircraft carriers. Here, look at the pictures. It sounds like a good proposition to me!"

"Let me see that article," I said.

Like most Mid-Westerners, my ideas of naval aviation were pretty sketchy. I knew that the Navy used seaplanes to observe battle practice, and that they had some large flying boats for patrol work, but as far as real flying was concerned, I had never given it a thought. That newspaper article opened my eyes a great deal. It seemed that the Navy had quite a large aviation branch, and that they were planning to expand it considerably. The Naval Academy was no longer able to fill all the vacancies, and there were now openings for graduates of civilian colleges and universities. This looked pretty interesting, after all.

"Where can I find out more about this?" I asked.

"At the nearest Naval Reserve Aviation Base," was the answer. "At Floyd Bennett Field, out at the foot of Brooklyn. Come along with me, and we'll drop out at the field during our lunch hour. Maybe we can both get in on this."

"Fine!" I agreed. "I want to see what this is all about!"

After a long subway ride from Manhattan to the end of the line, my friend and I caught a bus that finally brought us to Floyd Bennett Field. The driver let us out opposite a big hangar marked "U.S. Navy," and we walked over to the offices at the corner of the building. Inside, we were introduced to a Lieutenant Cutter, who invited us into a room marked "Pilots'

Ready-Room," passed us cigarettes, lit one himself, and made us feel at home right away.

"Have a seat," he said easily, "and I'll try to tell you a little bit about our outfit." He then outlined the Navy's offer. There was a month of preliminary training at one of the dozen Reserve Bases throughout the country, after which all students who soloed would be sent to the Navy's aviation training school at Pensacola, Florida, for a year of intensive training in all branches of service flying—seaplanes, landplanes, observation, scouting, patrol, and fighting planes. [Students now specialize in one of the above branches.] This was to be followed by three years of active duty with the fleet. Applicants from the New York area received their first month's training at Floyd Bennett Field.

"While you're in training," Lieutenant Cutter told us, "you'll be in the status of student officers. You have to be single, and agree to remain unmarried for four years."

My friend's face fell. "That lets me out," he said. "My wife would raise Cain if I went off and left her."

"Too bad," said Lieutenant Cutter with a grin. "We'd like to have you with us. How about you?" he asked me.

"I'm still a bachelor," I told him with a sigh of relief.

"Good. Now if you can meet the physical requirements, you shouldn't have any trouble. If you'll come with me, I'd like to have you meet the rest of the officers."

He then introduced us to the others, a sun-tanned, capable-looking, easy-going group who were a pleasure to meet. "You lucky stiff!" whispered my friend. "I'd give anything to be associated with a bunch of great guys like these fellows!

"How about it?" Lieutenant Cutter turned to me.

My mind was already made up. "I'd like nothing better,"

I answered, "and I'd like to put in my application right away."

"Fine!" he said. "I don't think you'll regret it."

After I had filled out several application forms, he told me that I could have a physical examination any time it was convenient to call at the Navy building in downtown Manhattan.

"Each month we start out with a new class of ten or twelve students," he told me. "The next class starts in August. If you qualify you can start in right away."

The die was cast. I might be leaving a good job with a real future, right in the middle of the depression, but at least it would be for something I'd had my heart set on for years. If I qualified, I would soon know whether or not I could fly, under the tuition of experts, in real airplanes.

CHAPTER TWO

Elimination Base

THE PHYSICAL EXAMINATION WAS SOON BEHIND me, and a few days later I was notified that I had been selected for the August Class at the elimination base. With eleven other candidates I reported for duty, and after being duly sworn into the Naval Service, we were assigned quarters in the administration building at Floyd Bennett Field.

The eleven other students were a likable bunch, most of them from eastern schools, and we were all enthusiastic about the prospects ahead of us. We were prepared for a good deal of military discipline, and were pleasantly surprised to find that the friendly, easy-going manner of the instructors was not merely a front assumed when talking to prospective recruits. "Make yourselves at home," Lieutenant Cutter told us. "These quarters aren't very comfortable, but we hope to have better ones soon. You'll start flying early each morning, so I'd suggest that you get plenty of sleep each night. If you like, you can go home on weekends."

The next day we drove down to the Brooklyn Navy Yard,

where we were outfitted in the uniforms of Marine privates—khaki slacks, shirts, and caps, under the supervision of a sergeant of Marines who also acted as our instructor in a half hour of infantry drill each day, Sergeant Sanborn.

Then the flying started in earnest. With three other students, I was assigned for instruction to a wiry, cold-eyed reserve lieutenant who sized us up with a critical eye and went straight to the point. "Come along with me and we'll look over the plane," he told us.

The plane was a Consolidated Trainer with a 250-H.P. Wright Whirlwind engine—the sluggish, dependable old NY landplane, with rubber bungee shock-absorbers and curved willow braces to protect the wing tips in one-wheel landings, but to me it looked like a lot of airplane, after some of the low-powered jobs on which I had been tempted to waste all my spending money.

"You're first," he told me. "Ever had any instruction before?"

"No, sir," I answered.

He showed me how to put on my parachute, and helped me into the plane. I wore a gosport type helmet, connected by a flexible metal speaking tube to a canvas mouthpiece which the instructor strapped over his face so that he had both hands free to grab the controls if I made the wrong move.

"I'll give you a short ride just to show you the characteristics of the plane," he told me. "Do you know what makes an airplane fly?"

I had a vague idea, but I shook my head.

"It's like skipping a flat rock across the water," he explained. "As long as the rock has momentum, it stays on the surface, and as long as an airplane has forward speed from the pull of the propeller, the flow of air over its wings provides enough lift to keep it flying. When the flat rock loses its momentum, it sinks to the bottom with a sort of spinning motion, and when the plane slows down to what we call stalling speed, the wings lose their lift, and the plane falls with a similar spinning motion, unless you nose it over to keep its flying speed above the stalling point. Get the idea?"

I nodded and he went on to explain further. "It's easy to get an airplane out of a spin if you have plenty of altitude, but if you let it stall close to the ground you may enter a spin before you realize it, which would be fatal. But even if the engine quits, you can keep your flying speed by nosing the plane over in a glide or spiral."

He then took off and climbed the plane to four thousand feet, where he put the ship through its paces, demonstrating stalls, spins and spirals. "Now you take it," he said, shaking the stick. He showed me how the rudder was controlled by the feet, while the stick moved the ailerons for banking and also controlled the elevators for climbing or gliding. I flew along awkwardly, while he tried to correct my more obvious errors. He coached me on my approach to the field, eased the plane down when I bounced high in the air after a wheel landing, and taxied back to the line to pick up the next student who eagerly awaited our return. Not until then did I notice the number 13 painted in big black letters on the yellow side of the plane. The date was August 13th, 1935.

The following day he went to work on me in earnest. Floyd Bennett Field was nearly a mile long, which gave him room to cut the throttle on me several times during the course of a take-off, simulating engine failure. The plane might be two feet in the air or twenty, when the throttle would be jerked back or the mixture control would be leaned out so that the engine would quit. A couple of times he even cut the switch on me. Whenever I failed to discover the source of the trouble immediately, he would yell in my ears through the speaking tube, "Well, do something! What's the matter with you? Are you going to sit there and wash this plane out? Nose over! You'll spin in and murder both of us!" Or when I leveled off for a landing with too much speed, he would cry, "Hold 'er off. Hold 'er off! Get her tail down! My God, don't make *all* your landings on your wheels! Here, let me show you how to land this airplane!"

Then he would take over the controls and demonstrate a landing so smooth that it made me green with envy, holding the plane just off the ground and easing the stick back until I could feel the plane lose flying speed just as the wheels and tail skid touched simultaneously. "There," he would say. "That's a three-point, full-stall landing. Now you do it."

But try as I would, I usually dropped in on one wheel, or tail first, or botched the approach completely. Once or twice he took me back to the line in apparent disgust before the hour was up, with various caustic comments. "That was the lousiest exhibition of thick-headed flying I ever saw. You'd better improve in a hurry, or it's back to the farm for you!"

And I would lie awake that night, haunted by the fear of "busting out" and returning in disgrace after only a month of training. But the next day would bring a new phase of the work, with steep spirals, recovery from spins, or spot landings on a little island sandbar in the bay. A word of approval from my instructor would make me forget all my previous errors, and everything would go along smoothly until I bungled an approach, when he would immediately read me the riot act. It finally grew so bad that I used to dread the approach of my daily period of instruction, and was always relieved when it was over. Then after we were back at the line and out of the plane, my instructor would pull a Jekyll-Hyde act that always amazed me, for he became a different person, quiet, cordial and friendly, explaining my errors and answering my questions until most of the difficulties were ironed out.

After about two weeks of this, he took me up one day for a general review, watched my work closely, and said cautiously, "You're coming along all right. Tomorrow I'll give you a final hour and then turn you over to the check pilots. If you get past them, you'll go to Pensacola."

That afternoon one of the other instructors turned the first student over to the check pilots. We all envied the lucky student who would be the first to solo, and congratulated him on his good work. He gave the first instructor a satisfactory ride, and went up for his final check immediately afterwards. We all stood around as he returned, waiting to see the instructor get out and wave him away for his first flight alone. But when he taxied back to the line he swung the tail around too fast, so that the wind caught it and carried him past the concrete warming-up platform towards the line of parked planes. The instructor managed to catch it with a blast of the propeller just in time to avoid hitting another plane and running down one of the mechanics. He turned and looked at the white-faced student as he cut the switch. "I'm sorry, son, but you're not ready to solo," he said slowly. "That was a good ride until you got in a hurry just now. You need some more instruction."

The effect of this episode on the rest of us was alarming. Until then we had all expected to get through the course after minor difficulties, but here was the most promising pupil, the one who had learned more quickly than any of us, who had failed to qualify. We all began to wonder, to lose confidence in our ability to fly. That night I had very little sleep. Tomorrow I would be up for my check. I was worried stiff. I could see myself going back to my old job, facing the questions of all my friends, having to admit failure at the one thing in the world I wanted to do more than anything else.

As I climbed into the cockpit behind my instructor the next day my face was set and my grip on the controls was tense. I *had* to make good—or else. Halfway across the field, the instructor chopped the throttle back. I nosed over so violently that he had to grab the controls to keep the plane from diving into the ground, and from then on I blew up completely. It was the worst ride I had ever given him. After half an hour of this he kept the plane on the ground and turned to me with a grim expression. "Listen, you big palooka," he said coldly. "If you don't settle down and cut out all this nonsense I'm going to bust you out of here and send you home with your ground-looping friend who nearly chopped up that plane yesterday. Now I'm going to give you just one more chance, and if you don't improve, you won't even *have* to ride with a check pilot!"

When we got back to the line after another workout only slightly better than before, he shook his head as he climbed out of the cockpit. "I don't know what's the matter with you," he said. "You've never been this bad before, but I've got to turn you over to the check pilots."

The first pilot to check me was Lieutenant Cutter, who climbed into the front cockpit with a grin. "Don't look so serious!" he said. "This is only a check—not a court-martial!"

Still tense and nervous, I took off and circled the field for a landing, badly undershooting my first approach on a field a mile long. After more bungled attempts, he kept me on the ground at one side of the field. "Let's take a blow," he said casually, lighting a cigarette while he watched me out of the corner of his eye. "You're trying too hard. Take it easy and relax. There's nothing difficult about this. Just forget I'm up here, and practice a few landings like you've been doing all week. You won't have any trouble."

Much reassured, I relaxed a bit and made several fair landings, while he coached me on my approaches. He even took over the controls to demonstrate for me a couple of times, while I grew more and more at ease. By the end of the hour, I realized that what he had actually given me was an additional period of instruction. "Your work is all right," he told me. "Now just give the next instructor who rides with you another ride like you've given me, and you'll be all set."

He made it appear so easy that I completely relaxed on the next check, and had no trouble at all. The check pilot had me make a few landings and a couple of spins, chopped the throttle on me once or twice, and told me to take him back to the line. As we swung around the field for our final approach, I noticed a blue and silver scouting plane taxiing down the center runway. The check pilot eyed it intently, while I swung farther to one side. Suddenly the plane on the ground veered sharply off the runway, dug a wing tip into the ground and ended up on its nose as the landing gear collapsed. The check pilot glanced back at me quickly. "Did you see that plane ground-loop?" he asked through the gosport tube.

I nodded in the affirmative.

"Well, don't forget it," he said. "That was a perfect object lesson in taxiing down-wind too fast. Take us on in."

Twice more he cut the gun on me as we crossed the field,
so that our last landing brought us back to the line. When I
taxied carefully in I could hardly believe my eyes as he
climbed out of the front cockpit. "Okay," he said. "Take her
away—she's all yours!"

My instructor, who had been waiting for me at the line,
grinned at me. "Nice work," he said. "Now, take it around the
field and make a landing just as you've been doing for me,
then come on back to the line."

So great was my relief at being alone in the plane with
nobody yelling in my ears, that I hardly realized I was soloing
at last. Following my instructor's orders literally, I swung
around the field just as he had taught me to do, cut the throttle
as soon as I was within gliding distance of the down-wind
edge, held the plane off the ground until the tail was down,
and came in with a fairly decent landing. It was so easy I was
pleasantly surprised. I had soloed! Not only that, but I was
the first one in my class to solo. Now I could return for the
congratulations of my classmates who were waiting their turn
at the line. I had never in my life felt more pleased with
myself.

Then it occurred to me that I had a very long way to taxi
back. I had landed at the extreme southeast end of the field,
and the warming-up platform was in the northwest corner
more than a mile away. Undaunted, I hugged the south end
of the field, taxying at a conservatively slow rate, meanwhile
keeping a sharp lookout for non-existent obstructions. After a
considerable delay, I approached the line, where the other
students and the instructors were waiting. My instructor came
forward to meet me as I climbed out of the plane. This was
the moment I had been waiting for. How fine it was to have

him the first to congratulate me! I tried to assume what I hoped would be a modest expression that befitted such a great occasion. Then I looked into a face that wore the most annoyed expression imaginable. "So you finally got here!" he said disgustedly. "Why didn't you land at Roosevelt Field and take a subway back!"

It was the blackest moment of my life. I crawled out of the plane and slunk off behind the hangar, and could hardly believe my ears when I learned that they had decided to recommend me for further training in spite of my unprecedented exhibition of cross-country taxying.

For once the elimination base did not live up to its name. All twelve of us in the August class soloed and received appointments as Aviation Cadets in the United States Naval Reserve, with orders to report to Pensacola for advanced flight instruction.

CHAPTER THREE
Pensacola at Last

WE WERE A HAPPY GROUP AS WE BOARDED THE
coastwise steamship that was to take us as far as Jacksonville.
All our friends came down to the ship to see us off, and the
farewell party they threw for us served to introduce us to
everyone on board. Jim Robb could play the piano, and Ray
McMahon had sung over the radio. Before we were out of
the harbor, Frank McGann had corralled a bevy of college
girls who were on their way back to school in the south. The
girls called us "the aviators" and we ate it up. After all, hadn't
we each logged ten full minutes of solo flight time? We took
over the ship for the duration of the cruise.

When the ship stopped over for several hours at Charleston,
the girls showed us around the historic old southern city, and
to some of us who had never before visited the South, the
change in tempo after the hurry and bustle of New York was

a revelation. The next day we left the ship at Jacksonville and boarded an air-conditioned train for Pensacola. So far, life in the Navy had been more than we had hoped for.

But as we approached our destination, vague misgivings as to what lay ahead began to trouble us. What sort of treatment could we expect? Would newcomers be hazed unmercifully, as we had heard was the custom at some military training centers? Most of us had submitted to this sort of horseplay in college, and we were all prepared to grin and bear it if necessary. At that stage, we would have risked the tortures of the Inquisition to get into a Navy airplane again.

As the train pulled into the station at Pensacola, we hurried out to crane our necks and scan the sky. To our disappointment, there were no planes to be seen. A taxicab driver appraised us with an experienced eye. "Take you out to the Air Station, Buddy?"

"Why—yes," we agreed, piling our luggage into the car and climbing in. "How far is the Air Station?"

" 'Bout seven mile," said the driver.

"Say, where are all the airplanes?"

The driver laughed. "This is *Saturday.* There's no flyin' around here on weekends."

"But what do the aviators—what does the Navy do on weekends?"

"Oh, they mostly plays golf, or swims, or fishes—all except those caydets."

"The cadets? What do they do?"

"They mostly raises hell, as near as I can make out. They're somethin' new that the Navy has just started up with. Folks down here calls 'em the Local Foreign Legion. Say, you fellows ain't caydets, are you?"

"Why yes, we are." We looked at each other, grinning.

"Oh," said the driver, shutting up like a clam.

The rest of the drive was made in silence. The cab driver took us through shady streets lined with palmettoes to the edge of the city, then out along the edge of a blue bay. After crossing a bridge over a bayou where porpoises were playing in the clear water, we were stopped by a uniformed Marine at the Air Station gate.

"Cadets reporting in," we told him.

"Check in with the O.O.D.," he told us.

The cab driver nodded, and drove us through a grove of live-oaks festooned with long grey streamers of spanish moss, pulling up to a stop in front of a building marked "Officer Of The Day."

The Officer Of The Day greeted us cordially. "Welcome to Pensacola, boys! You're the third class to report in. Give me a copy of your orders so I can log you in, and I'll call a car to take you over to the cadet barracks."

So far, no hazing. At the cadet barracks, we were even more pleasantly surprised. The cadet on duty at the entrance met us with a friendly handshake, introduced himself, and helped us with our luggage. He then showed us our bunks and issued us our bedding. "As soon as you get squared away," he said, "let me know and I'll show you how to get down to the beach. You might as well take it easy, for there won't be anything doing until Monday." With a reception like this, it was soon obvious that there was to be no "Hell Month" of hazing at Pensacola.

A short time later we were at Mustin Beach, walking across a soft, fine-grained sand that was as white as drifted snow. The water was clear and refreshing, and there were two diving towers with good spring-boards. Other cadets were swimming, diving, or lounging on the sand talking to attractive girls. Another cadet took us in tow. "Come on up to the Officers' Club, and we'll have a beer," he said.

"But we're not members," we said.

"You will be," he laughed, "as soon as you sign a chit!"

That's all there was to it. We simply signed our names to a chit for anything we ate or drank, and we automatically became members of the Officers' Club, with all of its privileges.

"This is swell!" we said enthusiastically.

" And that's not all," he said. "There are tennis courts, handball and badminton courts, and the best steaks and seafood you ever ate. And dances every weekend. There's one tonight. Come along with me, and I'll introduce you to some of the local girls. But watch out! There are some real honeys down here, and Pensacola is called the mother-in-law of the Navy!"

"Don't worry!" we laughed. "We're safe—we can't get married for four years!"

As the day wore on, we found even more to interest us. The dances were free, and so were the station movies, in an air-conditioned theatre. There were several motor launches available for fishing in the Gulf of Mexico, complete with tackle, ice-box, and crew, and the Gulf was alive with game fish. There was a well-equipped gymnasium, a football field, a baseball diamond, and a large basketball court. A stable of well-kept horses were ready for polo or riding over miles of bridle paths. Working hours were from seven to three, with a five-day week that gave plenty of time for us to take advantage of these excellent recreational facilities, which had been provided to keep us in good physical and psychological condition for the serious business of learning to fly the nation's war planes. The Navy had learned that adequate facilities for relaxation after the strain of military flying paid big dividends.

That night we danced under the stars on the terrace outside of the clubhouse at Mustin Beach, and returned to the barracks to climb into our double-deck bunks, where we slept like logs until noon the next day.

After a chicken dinner in the mess hall, we returned to the barracks to take stock of our surroundings. There were about two hundred cadets in the barracks, who had arrived in monthly classes of seventy. Nearly every state in the union was represented, so we had a cross-section of the country that brought a good many different viewpoints together. In spite of this, there was very little sectionalism, except for a little good-natured kidding by the California contingent, who insisted that the Florida orange-juice was pale, and referred to themselves as the A.E.F.—Americans Exiled in Florida.

Every eligible age was represented. In one bunk a cadet with a moustache, barely past the minimum age of twenty, tried to look old and experienced, while in the bunk above him was another who had barely squeaked in under the age limit. But there was one trait that all of them had in common, which was evident at once: an air of determination and seriousness about learning to fly. Many of them had resigned commissions as Army or Naval Reserve Officers to become cadets; some had left promising business careers; others had reluctantly parted from their fiancees, knowing that not one girl in a hundred would wait four years. Each one of them had faced the responsibility which he had accepted, and every one of them had made up his mind. You could see it in their faces. I began to understand what the taxicab driver had meant when he called them "The Local Foreign Legion."

But this term was not destined to apply to us much longer. Within a few months we were to see a definite change in the cadet battalion—a gradual molding of many individuals into a well-ordered group. We were to see the misfits, some few of whom are to be found in every large organization, quietly weeded out by the simple process of giving them enough rope to hang themselves, by their own breaches of the reasonably lenient regulations which had been devised by the officers in charge of our training. These officers were faced with the thankless task of indoctrinating us into the service as future naval officers, and they proceeded cautiously, carefully adapting the training program to meet the new problems which arose almost daily.

We were to learn that it was a simple matter to conform to these regulations, which were designed for the general welfare of everyone concerned, without suffering any loss of individuality or personal freedom. The occasional nonconformists who might have given the entire group a bad name were to eliminate themselves from the course in short order, and the others were to become part of the Navy. Although we did not know it at the time, we were to be in on history in the making, for during the next four years we were to see more changes in the Navy and in naval aviation than had occurred during the past quarter of a century.

CHAPTER FOUR

Primary Seaplanes

*"We joined the Nay-vee, to learn to fly.
And what do we fly? We fly an NY!"*
—SONG IN SQUADRON ONE

EACH CLASS WAS FORMED INTO A COMPANY OF
two platoons or wings, with one wing flying half of each day
while the other attended ground school. After a period of in-
doctrination in Navy Regulations, naval customs and terminology, practical seamanship, and military drill, we were assigned to instructors in Squadron One for our first flights.

My instructor was the exact opposite of the one I had at the
elimination base. This one was quiet, conservative, and never
raised his voice even after I had made some particularly stupid blunder. He took me down to the concrete ramp at the
edge of the beach to show me the airplane, which was the
same old NY-2, equipped with floats instead of wheels.

"You shouldn't have any trouble with these," he said re-
assuringly. "We do the same things you did at the elimination
base, only we have the whole bay to set 'em down on."

He started me off with a demonstration of the plane's handling characteristics, and I was surprised to find that the ideal

seaplane landing was not a smooth, gentle contact of the float with the water. Instead, he hauled the stick back until the plane's nose was high in the air, and we dropped in on the tail-end of the float with a resounding splash and a jolt that nearly shook my teeth loose. Every time I made a "hot" landing by coming in with excess flying speed and setting the plane down before it was fully stalled, he would say mildly, "Come on, now; you can do better than that! Get that stick back and make me a full-stall landing."

I liked his method of instruction, and the ten hours of dual work passed swiftly. He taught me how to taxi a seaplane, using the engine to turn out of the wind, and chopping the throttle to turn into the wind.

"A seaplane on the water is like a weathervane," he told me. "The tail always 'weathercocks' down-wind. If there is a strong wind behind you, don't try to taxi up to the beach, or you'll pile up the plane on the ramp. Just cut your gun, and the nose will swing into the wind. Then you can 'sail' the plane down-wind for a nice, easy beach approach."

He showed me how to take off and land in rough water, holding the plane nose-high on the take-off to keep the float from digging into the waves, and using a full-stall landing to set the plane down exactly where he wanted it. "In rough water," he said, "a hot landing is suicide. You'd plow into a wave and flip over on your back. With a full-stall landing you can pick your own wave and catch it at just the right moment."

I learned that in open water the crests of the waves always fell *into* the wind, and not down-wind, as they do in surf. My instructor pointed out the parallel "wind-streaks" in the water which always point into the wind, and showed me how to detect the direction of the wind from the shape of the ripples when there was only a light breeze. When there was no wind at all, he advised extreme caution. "When the water is glassy," he said, "look out, for it's dangerously deceptive. It's almost impossible to tell just how high you are above the water when there's no wind. You may level off twenty feet high, or you may dive in when you think you're yards above the surface. Under such conditions the only safe approach is the power stall. At night it's the *only* approach to use."

He then demonstrated a power-stall approach, keeping his throttle open just enough to let the plane down gradually at its lowest safe flying speed, and chopping the throttle as soon as he felt the tail of the float touch the water.

After a few hours of landings, he took me up several thousand feet and showed me how to recover from spins. Whenever I had a bad day, he would say, "That was pretty lousy, wasn't it?" and would laugh me out of my tenseness. Before I realized it, he had soloed me and passed me on to the more advanced stages, with flipper turns and "buoy shots"—spot landings alongside a buoy or marker beacon.

I began to relax a bit, in spite of the tension we were under from trying too hard. Every few days would see one or more of our class "busted out" and sent home. Each stage was followed by the inevitable check flight, and no student could pass on to the next stage until he had satisfactorily completed the check covering the preceding stage.

At the end of the check flight, when the instructor climbed out of the cockpit, he would wave to the timekeeper in the watch tower, thumbs up if the check was satisfactory, thumbs down if the student's performance was below standard. A student who got a "down" check on any phase had to fly two "up" checks, or he went before the Squadron Flight Board, a jury which included his instructor, the check pilot, the chief flight instructor, and the squadron commander. If the board considered the student's record good enough for him to get by with a bit of coaching, he was given a short period of "extra time"; otherwise he was referred to the Advisory Board, composed of the Station's senior officers. If the "Big Board" still turned down the student's request for extra time, he had to go before the station commandant, whose decision was final. Very few students received "commandant's time."

The result of this system was a nervous strain known as "checkitis," the symptoms of which were tenseness on the controls, a grim, do-or-die expression on the face of the student, and a set of compound jitters like those which had nearly eliminated me on my first check at the Reserve Base. Some check pilots could recognize these symptoms and put the student at ease immediately, but one or two who were known as "tough cookies" were inflexible and stern; the mere sight of their names chalked up on the blackboard schedule was often quite enough to make the student concerned start packing his trunk for home.

Two of our original group of twelve were eliminated in Squadron One. They came around to tell us goodbye with a forced levity that was all too transparent, for it was obvious that they were eating their hearts out on the inside. And their departure only made the rest of us more fearful. There were four more squadrons ahead of us. How could any of us ever hope to get through?

But there was no time to waste in idle worry, for there was plenty to keep us busy. Ground school occupied half of our working hours, and there was plenty of studying to do at night. Starting out with courses in ignition and engine theory, we progressed to practical work in the shops, overhauling engines under the expert supervision of enlisted mechanics who had spent years on aircraft engines. We had to tear down an engine and put it together again, then run it on the test stand. Then came the "trouble-shooting." After we had the

engine running satisfactorily, the mechanics would alter the timing, or flood the cylinders, or put the engine out of commission in any of a dozen different ways. We then had to find out what the trouble was and make the necessary adjustments.

Communications were a vital part of our training. Each day there was an hour of radio drill, sending and receiving Morse Code until we could pass the stringent requirements of the Radio Operator's Test. Visual Morse Code, or "blinker" practice, with a flashing light to show the dots and dashes, came next. We also had to pass a check in the use of semaphore flags.

In the assembly and repair department we went to the "sweat-shop," where we performed all the operations necessary in overhauling an airplane, re-covering, re-stitching, and "doping" the wings, checking the alignment of the rigging, and learning how to put the ship back together. This work was supplemented by classroom lectures on aerodynamics and navigation. In celestial navigation we learned how to "shoot the sun" with a sextant and to work out problems of latitude and longitude. In aerial navigation we were given problems in dead reckoning, with the additional complication of a movable base in the form of a theoretical aircraft carrier.

Those students who had studied engineering courses in college sailed through ground school with little or no trouble, but mathematics had been my weakest subject, and I spent many nights in the extra instruction classes while my more adept classmates went to the movies.

We packed parachutes and fired machine guns on the gunnery range. We shot service-type .45 automatics, and learned how to lead and follow-through with shotguns on the skeet range—invaluable training that was to help us later with aircraft gunnery. We spent hours at "wig-wag" practice with signal flags. We studied aerology—and got a practical demonstration in the form of a hurricane that interrupted flight operations for several days.

Steamers in the path of this tropical disturbance issued advisory storm warnings, and soon we knew that we were in for a real storm. The station had been in a standby condition, and when the word was passed, everything movable was battened down. The landplanes were flown north to a safe distance inland. Seaplanes were water-ballasted and lashed down securely inside the hangars. Motor launches and small boats were taken out of the wet-basin and secured on flatcars. The station was a scene of feverish but orderly activity, and long before the first telltale signs of the approaching storm were visible off the coast, everything was ready to weather a hard blow.

Hours before the wind came, the seabirds left. Beaches that had been dotted with gulls, pelicans, and shorebirds were now deserted. There was an ominous silence, broken only by the pounding of a heavy surf on the barrier island between Pensacola Bay and the Gulf of Mexico—in spite of the fact that there was *no wind*. The bay was glassy and the atmosphere oppressive. That night we knew that the center of the hurricane was east of us, for when the wind rose, it came from the north, although the storm was approaching swiftly from the south.

The wind increased slowly but steadily to a high-pitched, howling gale, accompanied by a driving torrent of rain. The old frame wooden building which served as a temporary cadet barracks rocked on its foundations, but the center of the disturbance luckily struck several miles east of us, and the air station escaped with only minor damage. The wind velocity at the "eye" of the hurricane was over a hundred knots, and as it tore its way inland it left an unmistakable trail: uprooted trees to the east of the vortex fell towards the north, while those a short distance west fell pointed towards the south. We did not forget that unscheduled lesson in meteorology for some time, and acquired a healthy respect for tropical weather disturbances.

Flight operations were suspended several days before and after the hurricane. The seaplane floats had to be drained and the crash-boats had to be taken off the flatcars and put back into the water. I fretted and fumed at the delay, for I had been ready to take the dreaded final check that was a review of all the work in Squadron One, and with each day's lay-off my chances of passing it dwindled. Finally we were ready to fly again, and after a short solo practice flight for a refresher, I started out with the check pilot.

As luck would have it, I drew the squadron's chief flight instructor for my check. Combined with the long lay-off, this additional mental hazard was too much for me, and I blew up completely. Before I was halfway through the check, I knew it was a "down," even though the check pilot gave me no intimation of his decision. But when I made a buoy approach and overshot the mark by fifty yards to "burn" the plane on in a hot landing, I knew what the score was. The check pilot then took over the controls to show me exactly what he wanted. I tried again, but it was too late to correct the bad impression I had made. When we taxied back to the ramp, he took me aside. "I'm sorry," he said, "but you're not ready for Squadron Two." My face showed my despair, for he grinned. "You need some more instruction here," he continued. "See your instructor and tell him I said to give you a review."

My instructor, Lieutenant Kershner, laughed when I reported the results of the check. "Don't take it so hard!" he told me. "Any extra time you get down here is just so much velvet. All you have to do is go out and fly a couple of 'ups'."

He soon ironed out the rough spots in my work, and the next day I was up for a check again, this time with the squadron's executive officer. He gave me a thorough working over, chopping the throttle when we were in a climbing turn, or taking me inland over the golf course and cutting the gun when there was barely enough altitude left to spiral back to the bay. This time I forced myself to relax, and at the end of the hour he gave me a non-committal "up" and turned me over to the next check pilot.

Halfway through the second check, the instructor cut the gun on me as we passed a point of land that jutted out into the bay. I nosed the plane over and headed into the wind. Ahead of us was a long area of shoal water that extended for some distance out into the bay. Our glide carried us farther ahead than the instructor had realized, so that when the plane's float settled down into the water we came to a grinding stop, fast aground on the sandy shoal.

My hopes sank. I expected to get credit for running us aground, but the instructor immediately took the blame. "That's one I misjudged!" he laughed. "Let me have the controls, and I'll try to get her off."

He opened the throttle, but the plane would not budge. He glanced around the bay for possible assistance, but the range boat was out of sight beyond the point of land. "It looks as if we're stuck until some other plane spots us," he said. "The tide's going out, and we may be here for hours."

I looked at the water, which appeared to be a little deeper behind us. "Maybe if I could turn us around, you could get us out," I suggested. "The plane would float a little higher without my extra weight."

"It might work," he said, "but how could I get back to pick you up?"

"I'll try to hang onto the float if you start moving," I answered.

"Go to it, if you don't mind getting wet!"

Stripping off my clothes, I climbed over the side and waded out to the left wing-tip float. While the instructor kicked hard right rudder and gunned the engine, I pushed on the float, and the plane slowly swung around until it was pointed downwind. Then I waded back and shoved on the main float while he rocked the plane back and forth with the engine wide open. The plane moved a bit, then started to slide along over the shoal. I grabbed a strut and hung on for dear life in the blast of the propeller. In a few moments we were clear, and I hauled myself back up into the rear cockpit. The instructor taxied out to deep water while I got back into my clothes, and once again we were off. He resumed the check, and after a few more simulated emergency landings he headed me back towards the squadron. "Your work is all right," he told me, "but I'm sorry I had to make you swim to prove it!"

CHAPTER FIVE

Ups and Downs

Oh, they march us in the Navy in the summer when it's hot;
And the rain it keeps us grounded in the winter when it's not;
And sometimes in the springtime, but mostly in the fall,
The wind it blows so blinking hard we never fly at all!
Chorus:
OHH, I'm fed up with Pensaco-la! I'm fed up with Pensacola!*
I'm fed up with Pensacola, and will be till I die!
(Air: Glory, Glory Hallelujah!)
— LAMENT OF CADETS IN SQUADRON TWO

BY THE TIME MOST OF OUR GROUP WERE
ready to go over to Squadron Two, the cadets had developed
a few traditions and an *esprit de corps* of their own. Naval
terminology began to supplant landlubber expressions: we
learned that a floor was a *deck*, a wall a *bulkhead*, and a drink-
ing fountain aboard ship was called a *scuttlebutt*, which was
also the term for unverified rumors. Upstairs was *topside*,
downstairs was *below*, and the ceiling an *overhead*.

Personalities, instead of being submerged by our close-knit

** My apologies to the Pensacola Chamber of Commerce. For "Pensacola"
substitute "Corpus Christi," "Coco Solo," "Honolulu" or wherever you
happen to be at the time. — R.A.W.*

organization, seemed to be even more emphasized. There were ninety-nine colleges and universities represented among 450 cadets, and each new class produced its own characters. The Navy runs to nicknames, which usually stick: Cadet West was inevitably dubbed "Mae"; Cadet Boeck, observed sitting cross-legged on an upper bunk clad only in his shorts, was known as "Buddha" from that day on; Cadet Campbell was named "Soupy." Others lost their first names, to become known only as "Pop" Noftsinger, "King" Lear, "Jungle Jim" Webster, "Hercules" Henry, "Fifi" Meili, and last but not least, the one-man crime-wave, "Horrible" Horrigan, who began his naval career by spinning in from 2500 feet at his elimination base and walking away from the crash, and whose other prodigious exploits in themselves would fill a book.

Then there was Cadet Vackert, who awoke one Sunday noon to find that sometime during the weekend he had unaccountably acquired an enormous set of Navy wings, tattooed in gaudy colors clear across his right shoulder, before he was halfway through the course. And Jim Robb, the first cadet to become a "German Ace" by destroying five American airplanes, without a scratch on himself. And Cadet Tammany, whose tear-gas fountain pen "accidentally" went off during the Executive Officer's tea-dance, clearing a couple of hundred guests out the Officers' Club in nothing flat.

Not a day passed without some interesting or amusing incident to make things lively. We lived so close together that nothing escaped us, and any minor discomfort we experienced due to overcrowding in the temporary barracks where we were quartered was more than compensated for by the friendships we made. Arguments were frequent but friendly; I do not recall anything but good-natured roughhousing among the members of that entire group during our year together.

Minor regulations had to be devised to keep us in hand from time to time. The descent of nearly five hundred sworn bachelors on a club dance, like some sort of a misplaced rodeo, was not without its complications. Any cadet who was short-sighted enough to bring his own date was lucky if he could dance ten steps with her before some grinning stag cut in. A club rule against cutting-in was the only solution. A few cadets rented apartments in town, living "ashore" and showing up only in time for morning calisthenics at *reveille*. Others rapidly followed suit, and in order to keep the barracks from being emptied, it was necessary to require us to be "aboard" on nights preceding flying days by 2230. (11:30 p.m. The Navy uses a 24-hour system of timekeeping.) A bunk-check insured our presence, and a demerit system was devised for those would-be offenders who didn't have sense enough to get a decent night's sleep before a day's flying instruction. We groused and grumbled, but most of us were usually in bed long before taps, except on weekends.

Crack-ups were frequent, but the cadets seemed to have charmed lives. During the first year's training of nearly half a thousand students, *not one cadet was injured.* Of course a number of planes were "washed out" completely, but the cadets always seemed to be able to walk away from the wreckage with nothing more serious than a few bumps and bruises. Considering the number of airplanes involved and the heavy aerial traffic around Pensacola, the Navy's flying course is one of the world's safest.

One cadet who made a hard landing in Squadron One turned in the following statement: "I landed and took off my goggles to clean them, and when I looked up the plane had sunk." The same cadet turned in this statement in Squadron Two: "I was flying along at 1000 feet when I heard a loud noise. I cut the throttle to see what was the matter, and when I looked up, my propeller was missing, so I came in and landed." Another cadet's engine quit while he was flying over a wooded area. He brought the plane down to a dead-stick landing in a clearing so small that the plane had to be dismantled before it could be removed. On another occasion, a cadet made a hard landing which damaged his plane so badly that the tail surfaces were held onto the fuselage only by the control wires. Blissfully unconscious of his predicament, he took off again and flew around for half an hour, finally bringing it back to the squadron only "because it steered so hard."

These incidents were typical of the minor crack-ups which occurred every few days. We knew that the Government had ten thousand dollars' worth of life insurance paid up for each one of us, but for over a year the law of averages did not catch up with us, and the Old Man With The Scythe forgot to exact his customary toll.

This was all the more incredible when you consider the type of flying we were doing in Squadron Two—small field work, aerobatics, formation, precision landings, and night flying. We were given eighty hours of flying in this squadron. Solo checks were made after seven hours of dual instruction, using the same old NY's we had used in Squadron One, equipped with wheels instead of floats.

It was here that we received our first formation instruction, elementary work that consisted of take-offs in section V, gentle turns in V or echelon, and shallow dives. Our introduction to night flying was equally simple. The instructors rode with us for an hour of familiarization, then turned us loose for a few

hours of solo work close to the field, and an hour or so of
practice landings in front of the big floodlights which made
the field almost as bright as day.

In Squadron Two I drew another "hardboiled" instructor.
"You're lucky you got him for an instructor," I was told, "for
he's the toughest check pilot on the station." This time I was
prepared, and when my instructor would rant and rave at my
awkward attempts, I sifted out the profanity and retained the
instruction. He taught me my first aerobatics, explaining the
reasons for these maneuvers. "You may have the mistaken
idea," he told me, "that stunting an airplane is done just for
fun or to show off. But if you stop to think, you'll realize that
we wouldn't even bother to teach you a lot of useless maneuvers, unless there was a damned good reason for it. Right?"

"Yes, sir," I admitted.

"Well, the main reason we teach you these aerobatic
maneuvers is to show you how to handle an airplane in any
attitude, so that you can recover from any unusual position
it might be thrown into by another plane's slip stream, violent
air currents, or losing yourself when the visibility is bad, at
night or in clouds."

Taking a pencil and paper, he sketched several diagrams.
"There are three kinds of aerobatic maneuvers," he continued.
"First there are the flying maneuvers, like the ordinary loop,
in which the plane is merely flown up, over, and around to
head in the same direction. Then there is the figure-eight,
which is simply a series of vertically banked turns around two
pylons. The wing-over is merely a figure-eight around two
points on the horizon. The Immelman turn is only half an
ordinary loop with a half roll at the top—a good way to head
your plane in the opposite direction."

With a model airplane he showed me how to go through the motions of each maneuver, as he went on: "Next there are the snap maneuvers, in which the airplane is whipped quickly into the desired position by suddenly moving the controls. For example, the barrel roll, or snap roll as we call it in the Navy, is performed by hauling back on the stick and kicking full rudder in the direction you want to go. Recovery is effected by using full opposite control. You use this same technique in recovering from a spin. Another snap maneuver is the split-S turn, which is also a convenient way to change your direction quickly: stall the plane by climbing steeply, haul back on the stick and kick hard rudder, and the plane flips over on its back. Dive out, and you're headed the other way. Here's another: if you're in a left flipper turn and want to change your heading, kick hard top rudder as you haul back on the stick, and the plane snaps up and over into a right flipper turn—a cartwheel."

He then held a sheet of paper by both edges and released both hands at once. It drifted to the ground with a rhythmic flutter from side to side. "That's the way a plane does a falling-leaf," he told me, "which brings us to the power-off maneuvers. You enter a falling-leaf just as you do a spin: cut the throttle, then stall the plane by climbing steeply, hold the stick all the way back, and kick full right rudder. As the plane starts to spin to the right, catch it with full left rudder, and continue using opposite rudder each time it starts to spin, keeping the plane on its original heading. When it's executed correctly, this is a very pretty maneuver to watch, but its main function is to help you find out a plane's spinning tendencies and show you how soon to apply opposite controls to recover from a spin. The spin is also a convenient maneuver in a dogfight, if you can make a precision recovery on a chosen heading. So you see that every stunt we teach you has a definite function in your flight training. But don't let me catch you trying any new ones of your own. No whip stalls, outside loops, or anything fancy. Whip stalls can rip your engine right off its mountings, and outside loops or outside flipper turns can easily tear off your wings, unless they are especially beefed up for it. Training planes aren't, so be careful."

After demonstrating each of these maneuvers several times, he showed me the correct way to make dead-stick approaches to a predetermined spot, using a 100-foot circle outlined on the ground, inside of which we were required to make full-stall, three-point landings.

After plenty of solo practice on this work, we came to the dreaded 25-hour check, Nemesis of many a would-be naval aviator. Three more of our original class of twelve were eliminated here, so that only seven of us were to win our Navy Wings.

We had worn parachutes on our daily flights for several months, but one weekend a couple of barnstormers came to town, advertising sight-seeing rides at a dollar a head, with a parachute jump as an added attraction. Like the postman who went for a walk on his day off, we went out to watch the exhibition. Since we had just finished a course in parachute packing in ground school, we stood around and kibitzed while the barnstormer packed his 'chute after the exhibition.

"We ought to make a jump some time," suggested cadet Turner, a Georgian, "just to know what to do if we evah have to bail out."

"How much to let us jump?" I asked the barnstormer.

"Twenty-five bucks," he answered, trying to get rid of us. Turner and I emptied our pockets, but even after we had appealed to the other cadets for a loan, the most we could scare up was nineteen dollars, mostly in ones and small change. The barnstormer saw that we were serious, and began to sit up and take notice when he saw the pile of bills. "Okey," he said, "make it twenty bucks and I'll do it."

Again we passed the hat, and managed to squeeze out the extra dollar in nickels and dimes. The barnstormer had two regulation parachutes, a 28-foot back pack and a 22-foot auxiliary chest pack to be used in case of emergency. "But I haven't got an extra ripcord," he told us. "If the first one who jumps drops the ripcord, the other can't jump."

We tossed a coin for the first jump, and I won. "You hang onto that ripco'd," Turner warned me, "or I'll drive home and make you walk back!"

I climbed into the front cockpit of the barnstormer's underpowered biplane, and we labored slowly up to what he told me was two thousand feet. The plane had no altimeter. I looked over the side, and even with my limited experience, I could see that we were over three thousand feet above City Field. The pilot motioned for me to climb out on the wing, and when he was satisfied that I could make the field, gave me the signal to jump. One look at the wind-streaks on the bay was enough to convince me that I would miss the field by half a mile, so I motioned for him to go ahead.

"What's the matter?" he shouted. "Lost your nerve?"

"No!" I yelled in his ear. "Take me up-wind. We'll miss the field!"

"You're crazy! Go ahead and jump, or you'll undershoot! And don't hit my stabilizer: I haven't got a 'chute!"

Bracing myself for a moment on the wing, I ducked under the stabilizer. It was easier than going off a diving board.

There was no sensation of speed or falling, rather a feeling of
being suspended in space. As soon as I was well clear of the
plane, I took a firm grip on the ripcord and locked my fingers
around it. A quick pull, and I felt a tremendous jerk that
snapped me into a sitting position, swinging under the wide
canopy of the opened 'chute. The ripcord was still fast in my
hand. Stuffing it inside my shirt, I looked below me.

The wind had already drifted me halfway across the field,
and I was still fifteen hundred feet in the air. Grasping the
risers on one side of the harness, I pulled the 'chute down
until it spilled air, to slip off some of my excess altitude. The
result startled me, for I dropped like a stone. When I let go
of the risers, the canopy snapped back into position and I
began to swing like a pendulum. I tried to stop these oscilla-
tions, but only swung all the harder. If I hit the ground at the
wrong end of such an oscillation, I knew it would be curtains
for my flying career.

Letting go of the harness, I tried to figure out which way
to pull on it to stop the swinging. To my relief the 'chute
steadied down of its own accord, just before I hit the ground
on the far side of the field. If I hadn't slipped off several hundred feet of excess altitude, I'd have landed in a grove of
tall pine trees.

Turner came rushing up to greet me. "Wheah's that ripco'd?" he demanded.

I brought it triumphantly out of my shirt, and together we
helped the barnstormer to repack the 'chute. A few minutes
later, Turner went up to repeat my experience. Again the pilot
misjudged his altitude, and Turner hit the ground in a drainage ditch, with the 'chute drifting outside of the field and
landing in the "blackjacks"—small scrub pine trees. Turner

also brought back the ripcord. We cheerfully paid over our twenty dollars, feeling that the experience was well worth every penny of it. If the naval authorities had learned about this escapade, we would probably have been dropped from the course. But if I ever have to bail out, the things I learned on that practice jump may come in mighty handy.

We spent nearly five months at Corry Field, learning the real fundamentals of flying in the yellow-painted primary trainers, which the advanced students derisively dubbed the "Yellow Perils." At first we were almost afraid to join the heavy stream of traffic around Squadron Two's half of the field, which we called "Suicide Circle," but by the time we were ready for our 25-hour checks we could set our ships down among the other landing planes with a fair degree of accuracy. The primary trainers, equipped with tail-skids and having no brakes, were required to land on the turf so that they could roll to a stop. After the 25-hour check we advanced to the NS, or Stearman Trainer, which was equipped with brakes and a tail wheel that permitted landings upon the circular asphalt mat in the center of Corry Field.

The change to these lighter, faster ships was every primary student's goal. We called them "the Yellow Fighters," and talked about nothing else for days after we were allowed to fly them. More instruction and a couple of weeks of solo practice brought us up to another check, as exacting in its requirements as the flight demonstration required for a commercial pilot's license. The final check, after 80 hours of intensive work, was a review of all we had learned in the squadron.

For my final check I drew an instructor who had given eight consecutive "downs" to my classmates. Before the flight

I spent ten minutes looking for him, only to find that he had been sitting in the plane for a quarter of an hour, waiting none too patiently for me to show up. He put me through my paces, with various caustic comments about my technique on

small field approaches, my diving wing-overs, and "square" figure-eights. I fully expected a "down," but near the end of the hour his manner changed. "That was a pretty good ride," he told me. "Now take me over to Felton's Farm and make four good circle shots, and we'll call it an 'up'."

We were required to make four three-point landings out of six approaches inside the circle for this check. I made only two, badly undershooting the others. The check pilot was reluctant about giving me a "down." "We'll call this check incomplete, on account of unfavorable wind conditions," he said. "I'll take you out again and we'll do it over."

The next day we repeated the check. "All right," he said, "now hit four out of six circle shots, and we'll call it quits."

This time I overshot five approaches. The check pilot

looked hurt. "I'm sorry," he said, "your other work is O.K., but I can't give you an 'up' with only three good circle shots out of twelve attempts."

My instructor was annoyed. "What's the big idea, letting me down this way?" he asked. "When I put a student up for a check, he can fly. Now you go out there and fly me two 'ups', or I'll kick you from one end of this hangar to the other!"

The next check was with Lieutenant Weir, a Marine instructor who was given most of the borderline cases. His record of checks looked like a submarine's log of ships sunk. The comment among the cadets in Squadron Two was: "Weir today, gone tomorrow!" This time I was really worried, but the first part of the check went off with very few comments, and when it came to the circle shots, I hit five out of six. It was the easiest check I had ever taken.

But there was still another check ahead of me. If I "busted" this one, I would have to go before the Advisory Board, with every chance of being dropped from the course. This time I drew a check pilot who was as notoriously easy as the others had been strict. Elated at my luck, I romped confidently through the check, made good all six of my circle shots, and taxied back to the circle with a broad grin to pick up the waiting check pilot. He climbed into the front cockpit and turned to face me. "That check," he said slowly, "was a nice 'down'." My grin faded. "Didn't anyone ever teach you to circle small fields until you got plenty of altitude after your take-off?" he asked. "During the last hour you constantly overlooked that little item. Why?"

I was desperate. I tried to think of some excuse, but was tongue-tied. He eyed me gloomily for a moment, then said,

"I'll tell you what I'll do. Take me back to Corry Field, and on the way back I'll give you one more chance to redeem yourself."

From Felton's Farm to Corry Field, ordinarily a five-minute hop, he cut the gun on me twelve times. We went down into every cow-pasture he could find. It was the worst workout I ever had, and when we finally got back to Corry Field I was wringing wet with sweat. As the check pilot climbed out of the front cockpit he stared at me coldly for a long moment. "Well," he said finally, "you just squeaked by."

CHAPTER SIX

Vought Corsairs

IT WAS NEARLY EIGHT MONTHS AFTER WE RE-ported at Pensacola before we reached Squadron Three. At last we could begin to breathe a bit easier for the first time, since failures at this stage of the course were rare. From Corry Field we were transferred to Squadron Three, whose operating base was a medium-sized field at one corner of the Air Station. Here we were to fly our first service-type airplane. This was the 02U, the reliable old Vought Corsair, with a 450-horsepower Wasp engine.

These planes made a tremendous impression on us, with their businesslike grey paint and their increased speed and power over the trainers we had been flying. We had great respect for their steeper glide and faster landings, and were delighted to find that they had a complete set of flight instruments in both cockpits. Up to this stage the student's cockpit had no turn-and-bank or airspeed indicators, so that we had been obliged to fly entirely by the feel of the controls. These newly acquired instruments gave us an additional means of smoothing out our airwork.

After only two hours of instruction in these planes we were

given a solo check that included more of the same circle shots that had nearly washed me out in Squadron Two. But to my pleasant surprise, I found that it was much easier to set these planes down where I wanted to land, and had no trouble in getting past the check. We were then given eight hours of solo practice to accustom ourselves to the increased stick forces that accompanied the two hundred additional horsepower in these bigger engines.

Most of this practice was conducted at Stump Field, which had a circle marked out at the intersection of two short runways. Landings made here were safe enough as long as we stayed on the runways, but the field itself was rough and pitted with deep stump holes, and at the south end of one runway there was a shallow pond. When the wind was from the south, an overshot landing required quick action on the student's part to keep from running into this pond, and the 02U engine had a bad habit of conking suddenly if we poured the soup to it a little too fast. As a result, hardly a week passed without some sort of a minor crack-up at Stump Field, and whenever the wind was from the southeast, the unlucky student usually had to wade ashore and leave his airplane nosed over in the middle of the pond, with its tail pointing ignominiously up towards the sky.

Early one fine spring morning, after about four hours of solo work in these planes, I was practicing circle shots at Stump Field. A light breeze from the southeast barely lifted the wind-sock, and I overshot my first two approaches. Overcorrecting on the third approach, I undershot slightly. As the plane began to settle, I eased the throttle forward to reach the field, and came squashing down in a hard landing that bounced the plane back into the air. I jammed on full throttle for a touch-and-go landing, but the engine choked up and began to sputter. The plane slowly settled back on the runway. I chopped the throttle back and stood on the brakes until the tail came up, but still the end of the runway rushed forward to meet me.

A few yards past the end of the runway lay the pond. In a moment I had reached the end of the runway and was bouncing across a series of huge stump holes, still with enough momentum to carry me straight ahead into the pond. As the wheels of the plane rolled into the water, the engine came back to life. Desperately I hauled back on the stick and eased the throttle forward to keep the plane moving. On I went, until the wheels were under water, but the propeller blast held the tail down, and before I realized it I was halfway across the pond.

Cautiously I opened the throttle wider, and the old 02U surged forward with its propeller throwing a great spray of mud and water in every direction, like a rotary snowplow running amuck through a swamp. I expected to nose over any second, but in a moment the spray subsided and to my amazement I found myself taxying out on the other side of the pond, dripping mud and water from every wire and strut. Carefully taxying around a dozen deep stump holes, I circled the pond and headed back for the safety of the runway. My knees were shaking and I could hardly believe my good luck. A few yards more, and I could take off again, with no one the wiser except myself.

Twenty feet from the runway, the right wheel slipped into a grass-covered rut, and I felt the nose drop. I chopped the throttle back, but it was too late. The plane's tail rose slowly and majestically into the air, the propeller bit into the soft dirt and stopped, and there I sat, nosed over within spitting distance of safety. For a moment I was unable to do anything but sit there with my mouth open, but the pungent odor of gasoline fumes snapped me back with a start. Gasoline was dripping out of the up-tilted fuel tanks and running down over the engine; I could hear it sizzle as it dripped onto the hot exhaust stacks. One word filled my mind: *F I R E!*

Tripping my safety belt, I scrambled out of the cockpit, jumped to the ground, and galloped off to be out of the way of the explosion. Nothing happened. The plane sat there with its tail in the air. I crept cautiously back, ready to run at the first burst of flame. Still nothing happened, so I reached timidly into the cockpit, turned off the fuel valves and cut the ignition switch.

A plane overhead circled the field, and the pilot headed back towards the squadron to report the accident. A wave of shame flooded over me. I had never been more embarrassed in my life. Here I had wrecked an airplane, through a stupid blunder in technique that I had been repeatedly warned against. I felt like crawling into a hole and hiding.

Soon another plane appeared, and after it landed and taxied up to me, the squadron engineering officer stepped out. He inspected my plane critically for a moment, then turned to me. "All you need is a new prop," he said. "This one is only slightly bent and can easily be straightened. But how in the devil did you manage to get all that mud on the plane?"

"I got that going through the pond."

"Going through *what?*"

"Through the pond," I repeated, pointing to the pond at the end of the runway.

"Wait a minute! What are you trying to give me? Don't try to tell me you went through that pond!"

"Yes, sir," I insisted. "Look, here are the tracks."

Even when I showed him the plane's wheel tracks, heading straight for the center of the pond and emerging wet and muddy from the opposite side, he could hardly believe it. "I've seen a lot of airplane tracks going into that pond," he said, "but this is the first time I ever saw any tracks coming out the other side!"

A truck soon arrived with a couple of mechanics and a spare propeller. We changed the prop, eased the tail down to the ground, and started the engine. After the mechanics checked it for vibration and gave it their O.K., I climbed in and flew it back to the squadron. On the way back all my old fears returned. Would I be grounded? Would they give me a special check and send me home? I was worried stiff. As soon as I landed, the Squadron Duty Officer called me in. "Were you in Number Seventeen the last hour?" he asked.

"Yes, sir," I answered, expecting the worst.

"That hop was incomplete," he told me. "You're to take Number Twenty out and finish the hour."

"Yes, sir!" I replied, starting off at a run.

"Come back here!" he called. "One thing more: try and keep this one out of the water. You left seaplanes six months ago."

"Aye, aye, sir!" I answered, saluting.

He grinned and walked off.

That bent propeller was the only damage chalked up against me during the entire course at Pensacola and for two years afterward. The next time I nicked a prop, it nearly cost me my neck. But of that, more later.

After another uneventful check, I went ahead to the next stage—formation work. Three of us were sent out to practice our section work, and then we were assigned with two other sections to a nine-plane formation for division tactics. (Operating squadrons attached to aircraft carriers in the fleet are composed of two divisions. There are three sections to a division, and three planes to a section. These terms will be used from now on in this book to denote operating units.) Here we learned the geometric precision and rhythmic timing that make well-executed formation maneuvers a source of endless satisfaction. We learned parade formations, including the division V, copied from the cruising formations of wild geese, and the division line, with all nine planes lined up on the leader, wing tips almost touching. We shifted from the maneuverable echelon of V's to the division echelon, ideal attack formation that permits planes to peel off at split-second intervals in vertical dives. An instructor cruising above us in a fighter took detailed notes on our execution of various maneuvers, for constructive criticism at the end of the hour. This was teamwork combined with speed, precision, and power under control. Formation work taught us air discipline—the most important factor in military flying, upon which individual safety depends when mass maneuvers are involved.

After two weeks of division formation in the O2U's we were checked out in the SU (Vought Scout), a heavier, faster scouting plane with a 650 horsepower Hornet engine. These ships weighed about two tons, and since we were instructed to glide them at 70 knots in order to keep them well above stalling speed, overshot landings were frequent. At first it was a common sight to see three or four planes out of a nine plane division making two and sometimes three passes at the field before they all came safely down, but after a few hours of practice we were able to make the field on the first try.

In the SU's we had a chance to try out the radio code we had been practicing daily for over half a year in ground school. Up until this stage, radio practice had been drudgery, but now we got a real kick out of being able to send messages from plane to plane and to keep in touch with the squadron's base radio station while cruising a dozen miles away. Gradually the apparently unrelated phases of the training syllabus began to make sense, and we were able to see good reasons for a number of courses which had seemed useless to us in ground school.

Radio formation was followed by a stage everyone had been impatiently awaiting: aircraft machine-gunnery. Using a cloth sleeve towed by another plane for a target, we blasted away at it from the rear cockpit with free-swinging machine guns. For the first time we had the thrill of shooting real bullets at a flying target, and of marking the sleeves afterward to see if we had made any hits.

Even more fun was the camera gunnery. An instructor in a fighter would attack from the rear, while we "shot" at him  from the rear cockpit with a machine gun taking pictures instead of firing bullets. This was the most exciting game I had ever played. While the pilot up front attempted to dodge our pursuer, I swung the gun on its mount from side to side, trying to keep the zooming, diving, elusive fighter in my gunsights, and the gale that whipped back from the propeller shook me from one side of the cockpit to the other. This was high adventure, worth all of the preceding months of strain and uncertainty.

The instructor who flew the target plane for our camera gunnery took great delight in hanging his little fighter directly beneath the firing plane and following every movement that the student pilot made in his efforts to get away. It was no easy matter to swing the heavy machine gun from one side of the cockpit to the other, trying to get a few shots before the target plane dodged over to the other side. Finally my pilot managed to get me in a position where there was a good opening, and I blasted away with all the film in my gun at the annoying "enemy" plane, which stuck on our tail like a buzzing gadfly.

In my mind's eye I could almost see the bullets ripping through his gasoline tanks. Then the target plane zoomed out

of range and the "fight" was over. And when the films were
developed, I found that I had plenty of hits, but not quite
the kind I had expected: the tail surfaces of an airplane were
neatly outlined in the center of my gun sights, but it was my
own plane. According to the irrefutable photographic evi-
dence that was before me, the airplane which I had shot
down in my first aerial dogfight was the one in which I had
been flying.

It was hard to believe that the toughest part of the course
was behind me, but when I finally was able to realize that I
now had a pretty fair chance of completing the course, I
began to relax and to enjoy life a little more. Some of the
other students in my group carried this relaxation a bit too
far. One student who was reported for low flying over a farmhouse was about to get off with a reprimand, until it was
discovered that his plane had a neat pattern of bird-shot
through the lower wing. He was grounded for ten days.

Another student, flying on a cross-country navigation hop,
lost his map over the side. His wingman, seeing the map
blow away in the slip stream, handed his own map to the student observer in his rear cockpit, and the observer decided
to pass the map over to the first plane. Taking off his parachute, he walked out on the wing, while the observer in the
other plane walked out on his own plane's wing to meet him.
The two pilots flew along with their wing tips almost touching, while their observers tried to pass the map from one
plane to the other. Finally one of the pilots became jittery
and signaled for his observer to come on back. The observer
shook his head in refusal, insisting on another try. The pilot
then took matters into his own hands, and kicked the plane
into a steep wing-over. The observer held onto the wing strut

for dear life, then crawled back, white and shaken, into the rear cockpit. That ended the wing-walking activities for a while.

When I look back on some of the crazy chances we took at that stage of the game, it makes me shudder. Everytime we went out alone or in formation without an instructor along, we immediately took the opportunity to do all kinds of wild flat-hatting, looping the old obsolete crates in section formation, dogfighting until we "blacked out" our observers in the rear cockpits, or chasing automobiles off the highways. Then one day we received an object lesson that put the fear of justice into us. A group of students flying along on a navigation flight, thinking that they were unobserved, separated for the customary hedge-hopping. Meanwhile the leader changed course, and when the others climbed back to rejoin him, he was nowhere in sight. The wingmen straggled back at half-hour intervals, and the whole group was grounded. After this incident, a chase-pilot was assigned to follow each cross-country formation, which quickly put an end to our derelictions. There is a strange providence that sometimes watches over fools, drunks, and over-confident, under-experienced student aviators. This guardian angel must have been working overtime while we were going through Squadron Three, for we sailed through this phase of our training without a single serious accident.

CHAPTER SEVEN

Seaplanes Again

TEN "DON'TS" FOR NAVAL AVIATORS

I. Don't try to take off or land down-wind.
II. Don't fool with the weather.
III. Don't accept a plane for flight without careful inspection.
IV. Don't attempt any restricted maneuvers.
V. Don't try to fly into the overcast before you get an instrument rating.
VI. Don't practice aerobatics without plenty of altitude.
VII. Don't try to be the *boldest* flier, if you want to be the *oldest*.
VIII. Don't stall!
IX. *Don't stall!!*
X. DON'T STALL!!!

—ANY GOOD FLIGHT INSTRUCTOR

AT ONE TIME OR ANOTHER, I'VE VIOLATED most of the admonitions listed above. And almost without exception, the result has immediately spelled *trouble*. Most student fliers pass through a reckless stage in which they overrate their flying ability and find themselves in serious difficulties. Nothing is quite so dangerous as this over-confidence, which leads students to attempt the impossible. Far too frequently, the flier who violates the elementary rules of air safety isn't around after such a mistake to profit by his experience, but if he lives to tell about it, a good healthy scare will usually make a Christian out of him for a long time afterward. I received such a scare shortly after I reached Squadron Four.

The transition from service-type landplanes back to seaplanes was made much easier by the use of the same 02U's we had been flying in Squadron Three, equipped with floats for water operations. A short period of familiarization under the guidance of an instructor gave us the feel of seaplane landings again, and we were all set to start our instrument-flying course. This important phase of our instruction preceded all our other work in Squadron Four, where the training syllabus included three-place torpedo planes, catapult take-offs, and horizontal bombing from the "Big Boats"—twin-engine patrol-bombers that weighed nearly six tons.

During the last stages of the instrument-flying course, we were sent out to practice in pairs—one student under the hood in the forward cockpit, and the other in the rear cockpit to act as safety pilot. The heavy 02U seaplane was ideal for this "blind flying," because of the stability given to the ship by its ponderous float. We were instructed to glide it at eighty knots, at an angle which may best be described as a gentle dive, for at that stage of the game our instructors were taking no chances on our stalling in a slow glide and spinning into the bay.

One fine summer afternoon another student and I were sent out to practice our instrument work together. There was a brisk southwest breeze. Mac, the other student, was at the controls in the forward cockpit, and we had both worn our gosport helmets so that we could talk to each other through the speaking tubes.

As we circled the bay I noted idly that the tide was running out, as there was a white line of disturbed water moving westward to the mouth of the bay, with a vivid contrast between the dark brackish water of the bay and the brighter green water of the Gulf.

Ordinarily one circuit of the bay took more than a quarter of an hour, but a white cloud to the northeast had encroached on part of our area and we were forced to cut our circle short. The next time around, the trip took even less time, and it was soon evident that the white bank of cloud was moving toward the southwest, in spite of the surface wind. I looked at it closely, but it seemed harmless enough, and down below me I could still see the big boats and torpedo planes taking off and landing into a southwest wind.

However, on the next circuit, the white cloud-bank had crowded all of the planes at our altitude close together in the western end of our area, and it was obviously advancing even farther. I thought of returning to the base, but Mac's time was not up, and I was enjoying the ride.

Looking around at the other instrument-flying planes, I saw that one was heading for home, another was spiraling down towards the bay, and the third was still circling in the remaining clear space.

I studied the white cloud-bank for a moment. It looked soft and downy like a powder-puff instead of the smooth, oily, rolling surface of the Gulf thunderheads which I knew were bad medicine. Curiosity overcame my better judgment, and I decided to investigate the cloud. Mac was under the hood; he'd never know the difference, even if I couldn't see. "Turn northeast," I told him, "and hold your altitude."

The plane slid into the gleaming white mass and all sense of motion ceased. The intensity of the light was almost as great as on the outside, yet the wing tips were barely visible. It was like flying through fine snow. At first the plane cruised almost as smoothly as before, but in a short time it began to roll and pitch. Suddenly I realized that if Mac should lose control of the plane, hampered as it was by the cumbersome float, we would spin down through the cloud without a chance of regaining control before we struck the water.

"Turn left!" I said, as calmly as I could. "Fly southwest!"

Obediently Mac started his turn. I watched tensely as the compass began to swing. The ship bucked and yawed, throwing the compass into temporary confusion. Mac fought the controls for a moment, then spoke through the voice tube: "It's getting too bumpy for me to handle her in here. You'd better take her over for a minute, while I rest up a bit."

Panic seized me as I answered: *"Whatever you do, don't let go of those controls! Stay under the hood, and try to keep her level!"*

I could feel the plane lurch as Mac realized with a start that the control of the ship depended on the instruments in his cockpit, and that he was now actually flying blind, without any help from me if he made any mistakes. For a long time he held his course, until finally we burst out into clear air.

"All right," I said weakly, "you can come out now."

The hood was jerked open and Mac's head popped out, staring first at the cloud-bank and then glaring at me.

"What's the big idea?" he yelled. "Taking me into that

soup! Wait till I get you down on the ground!" He nosed the plane over and headed back towards the station.

Looking back at the cloud-bank, I saw that underneath the rim it was dark and threatening. Beneath us, all the training planes had vanished from their practice area, but the wind streaks on the water were still from the southwest. The disturbed water that marked the line of the tide-rip was more pronounced than ever, and was moving visibly faster than before. A vague, uneasy feeling of having forgotten something oppressed me, but I dismissed it as a product of the scare my foolhardy excursion in the clouds had given me.

Even though I was anxious to get back to the base, the trip across the West Bay seemed unaccountably short. As we approached our destination, Mac swung the ship inland over the watch-tower, glanced at the wind-sock to be sure that the wind was still from the southwest, eased his throttle back for the approach over the hangars, and started his glide towards the water. Looking ahead, I saw that the tide-rip had apparently kept pace with us, and was now right underneath us. Then I suddenly realized what it was that I had forgotten. *The tide had gone out over an hour ago!*

For some seconds the meaning of the disturbed line of water did not dawn on me, until Mac chopped the throttle and eased the stick back for a landing. Then some instinct prompted me to commit the cardinal sin among aviators: I grabbed the stick away from him and slammed on full gun.

Mac told me afterwards that at first he was too angry to protest, and then too amazed at the results to say anything, for the ship swept across the bay at such a rate that we were a mile from the hangars before I could turn the controls back over to him. We had been riding on the crest of a 180-

degree change in the direction of the wind, so that our approach into what we thought was a ten-knot wind from the southwest was in reality *down-wind* on a 50 knot gale from the northeast.

Nor were we alone in our mistake. A nine-plane division of landplanes, circling Station Field for an approach, was caught just as the wind shifted, and the planes barely managed to clear the trees on the down-wind side as they were swept across the field. We saw them flash past overhead, fighting to get back around into the wind, as we taxied up to the beach in the lee of our hangars.

Off to our right we watched another seaplane, which had been circling the bay after a catapult take-off into the southwest wind. It leveled off for a landing along the seawall next to the catapult, went through the motions of landing, and rolled up into a ball right before the eyes of the horrified catapult crew, who were relieved to watch the pilots swim away from the wreckage unscathed.

One of the instrument-flying planes was still unreported, but a few minutes later the crash-boat came alongside and the two pilots, wet and dripping, came into the hangar.

"Where's your airplane?" we asked them.

"At the bottom of East Bay," they replied glumly.

"What happened?"

"We landed along the wind-streaks, but they were pointing the wrong way!"

"We nearly did the same thing," said Mac, "only in our case it was the wind-sock. I could have sworn it was pointing the other way."

"It was," someone told us, "but it swung directly around just as you leveled off for your landing."

From that day on, I became suspicious of wind indicators in general. Too often, I learned, the rotating wind T's and similar mechanical gadgets jam, or go out of order, or have a dangerous lag. Smoke, dust on a field, or wind-streaks on the water are much more to be trusted than any man-made device for showing the direction of the wind. And I have never forgotten the peculiar, instinctively uneasy feeling I had that day when I saw the water glide by beneath me much too fast for a normal landing. Anyone who has almost gone through with a down-wind landing will not forget the sensation.

Upon completion of the instrument-flying course we were checked out in the heavier, sluggish TM's and TG's—torpedo planes mounted on twin floats, equipped with a yoke or wheel control in place of the conventional stick. In these planes we carried a half-ton dummy torpedo, skimming along just above the wave-tops and making practice drops that sunk countless imaginary enemy battleships. Instead of having a single float or pontoon in the center and smaller floats on the wing tips like the observation seaplanes, the torpedo planes were equipped with twin floats. In rough-water take-offs these big floats would hit the waves with a jolting motion that shook the whole plane, and a ride in the third cockpit back over the tail was a rough experience. My instructor, Lieutenant J. C. ("Jumping Joe") Clifton, used to say that the TM seaplane had the world's roughest rumble seat.

The military function of these big torpedo planes conjured up exciting mental pictures. We could easily imagine how the pilots must feel in war-time, cruising along behind a smoke-screen in a stepped-down formation while the leader stuck his head up over the protecting screen for a momentary glimpse of the enemy battle line, then diving through the smoke-screen in unison at a given signal, levelling off only a few yards above the water and trying to steady down so the gunners could get off their deadly "tin fish" before the enemy could open fire. That kind of flying would really take guts! A few feet too low, and the splash of the torpedo would strike the tail surfaces of the plane and dive it into the water. A few feet too high, and the torpedo might plunge in too steeply, shoot out of the water like a leaping porpoise, and hit the plane that had dropped it. This would be ticklish flying, calling for split-hair judgment, with no nerves in the face of concentrated machine-gun fire and muzzle-burst shrapnel from the enemy anti-aircraft batteries.

After torpedo planes we went to the Big Boats, learning a new technique of sailing and taxying these gargantuan monsters, which handled almost as easily as airplanes one-tenth their size. I had not expected to enjoy patrol plane instruction, but the new problems that accompanied multi-engine operations fascinated me. I learned that by using just one engine to taxi the big planes, I could spin them around almost on a dime. For this reason, beach approaches seemed easier than they had been with even the primary seaplanes, and we could spot these seemingly clumsy giants into an opening not much wider than their wing-span.

At first it was strange to have two sets of engine controls—individual throttles, switches, and mixture controls for each engine. But soon we grew used to handling both throttles with one hand, changing their settings minutely to synchronize the engines. Unless the propellers were properly synchronized at exactly the same engine speed, we could hear a loud "Wah, wah, wah!" which grew faster as the difference in R.P.M. increased, to a "Wah-wawa-wawawah!" and decreased as we attuned them to the same speed: "Wawawa-wa-wah-wah, wah, waah!" until there was no fluctuation in the sound. The check pilots had ears which were very sensitive to this sound made by the propellers when they were out of phase, and the slightest suggestion of a "Wah wah" was enough for them to give us a low mark on a check.

On the checks they might cut one throttle or both, to simulate an emergency power failure. When only one engine was stopped suddenly, the big boats would slew around in a violent skid that required both feet on the rudder bar to keep the nose straight. This made the work even more interesting. Sitting there between the two throbbing engines and feeling the sense of tremendous power under fingertip control soon got under my skin, and I decided that if I ever had a choice for active duty, the Big Boats would be first on my list.

Horizontal bombing from these planes proved to be just as exciting as free-gunnery. Our target was a real battleship, the old USS Massachusetts, which had been stripped and used as a target for the harbor defense guns years ago. The rusty hulk, with her superstructure half out of the water, now lay at the entrance to Pensacola Bay, and made an ideal target for our heavy practice bombs. Our bombsight was an electrical brain which calculated air-speed, drift, and altitude, directing the plane and releasing the bombs with uncanny accuracy when we were so high that the big wreck looked like a pin-point. Any doubts I had about the effectiveness of modern horizontal bombing vanished promptly.

The last training phase of Squadron Four was catapult familiarization. In my opinion, there is no more outrageous sensation that can be experienced than that of a catapult "shot." During the first one that I sat through, I surely thought the world had come to an end. One minute I was sitting in the rear cockpit of the O2U seaplane that was clamped on the end of the catapult, watching the preparations below me. I saw the catapult chief open the breech of the firing mechanism and shove home a five-inch shell nearly a yard long, filled with smokeless powder. I felt the plane shake and strain as the pilot in front of me opened his throttle wide, and braced my head against the pad behind me. Out of the corner of my eye, I saw the chief jerk the lanyard. Then time seemed to stand still—an unearthly sensation of rigid immobility and suspended animation. An instant later I found myself flying along as normally as from an ordinary take-off.

Those were my impressions from the rear cockpit. For some reason the sensations from the front cockpit were not half so startling, but I got a tremendous kick out of it just the same, even on the third and fourth shots, and felt that a more satisfying climax to our training in Squadron Four could not have been devised.

CHAPTER EIGHT

The Dive Bombers

BY THE TIME WE REACHED SQUADRON FIVE, everyone took it for granted that we would be able to finish the course, and a much more easy-going attitude prevailed all around. Ground school was behind us, and we spent the whole day at the squadron. There were only seven instructors in this squadron, which seemed strange to us until we found that they could check a student from the ground while he slow-rolled his fighter half a mile above the hangar, and tell whether he was slipping or skidding. Instruction in this squadron was just hearsay; they could tell us what to do, but they couldn't ride with us and show us how to do it. We were flying single-seaters.

The Skipper, Lieutenant Commander J. R. Tate, went out of his way to make us feel at home. "Over here," he told us, "we try to run things just as they do in an operating squadron out in the fleet. Keep your eyes open, don't take any chances, and we'll have you out of here in a few weeks. But the first one of you who runs into a boundary light, I'll personally snatch him bald-headed and send him to the commandant for a one-way ticket home!"

With this informal introduction to the squadron, we immediately relaxed. My flight class included a dozen other cadets, five Marine Corps Lieutenants, and a Coast Guard officer.

We started to work immediately. An instructor gave us a lecture on the handling characteristics of fighting planes, then took us out to one of the little single-seaters to go over the instruments in the cockpit. Here was one airplane where we had to make good on the first try, for there would no longer be an instructor in the front cockpit to take over the controls if anything went wrong. With this realization, all our hearts began to beat a bit faster. The planes were Boeing Fighters (F4B-1's) and after the giant patrol planes we had been flying, they looked no bigger than mosquitoes.

I'll never forget that first flight in a fighter. Taxying out on the runway, I eased the throttle forward, intending to make a conservative take-off. Before the throttle was halfway open, I was astounded to find that the plane was fifty feet in the air and climbing with no apparent effort. I started what I thought was a gentle bank, and the little plane yawed widely as I over-controlled. I straightened out fearfully, and timidly applied a bit of pressure on the rudder. The plane went into a violent skid. I eased back on the stick, and a sudden zoom carried me upward a couple of hundred feet. These planes were really touchy!

At first I over-controlled badly until I found that this plane could really be flown with the fingertips. I stuck my left hand out into the slip stream to see how strong the wind felt, and to my amazement the little ship immediately went into a gentle left turn. Experimenting further, I found that I could actually turn the ship in either direction with the wind-resistance from my outstretched arm. I had expected these planes to be sensitive on the controls, but this was incredible. It responded to the slightest touch. All I had to do was lean one way or the other when I wanted to turn, and the little plane responded as if it had read my mind. It was almost like having a personal set of wings. I looped, dived, zoomed and spun the little ship around the sky, feeling it out and growing more delighted each minute with the way it handled. All thoughts of Big Boats or any other airplanes were forgotten; at last I was really flying!

After an hour of the most exhilarating flight I had ever known, I remembered with a start that I still had to get the plane back on the ground. Fighter landings were supposed to be pretty tricky. With some trepidation I circled the field, eased the throttle off, and started my approach. The little plane settled like a bit of thistle-down, with perfect control all the way, and seemed to land itself. The landing wasn't even fast, and the plane rolled only a short distance after it touched the ground. It was easier to fly than any airplane I had ever flown. My mind was made up: from that day on, I never would be satisfied flying any plane but a single-seater.

We were given several hours of familiarization airwork and landings, and then went on to the more advanced stages. In precision landings we practiced power-off landings over an obstruction which could be dropped if we undershot. This was called "skipping the rope," and in these approaches we found that by conserving our altitude and slipping it off at the last minute we could set the little fighters down in a very short space.

Stunt checks were complicated by the addition of a time element. We were allowed five minutes to complete a series of loops, double snap rolls, Immelman turns, slow rolls, precision spins, and rolls on top of a loop. The last-named maneuver is a high-speed loop in which the airplane is snap-rolled completely around as it reaches the inverted position, so that it emerges on its original heading. When properly executed, this is a beautiful maneuver to watch, but I had a lot of trouble with it, either going into an inverted spin when I was too slow, or snapping the plane through a roll and a half at the top of the loop to come out of the maneuver headed in exactly the opposite direction—a sort of a fancy Immelman turn.

Another maneuver that startled me the first time I tried it was the slow roll. The first time I rolled the plane over on its back and hung head-down suspended only by the safety-belt I was terrified, and immediately pulled out in a dive. After a few more attempts I managed to go through the motions, and then I enjoyed the sensation. It was fun to point the plane's nose at a cloud on the horizon and slowly rotate the wings through a complete circle while I tried to keep it headed for the cloud, and I began to feel pretty cocky about my ability, until the instructor who checked me took all the wind out of my sails. "Well, you got by," he told me, "but I think you've discovered a new maneuver. That's the first time I ever saw a slow roll combined with an S-turn."

A friend of mine was the first cadet to join the Caterpillar Club, when his fighter went into an inverted spin while he was practicing slow rolls over Perdido Bay. He fought the plane down to a thousand feet in an unsuccessful effort to bring it out of the spin, then tripped his safety-belt and took

to his parachute. The plane spun on down, while the pilot
landed in the bay, where he managed to keep afloat by tying
the legs of his khaki trousers together, scooping them full
of air, and using them for water-wings until he was picked
up by a seaplane.

Formation work followed. We now made landings as well
as take-offs in V formation. Our division formation work advanced to "slide-over" turns, which allowed us to maneuver
a division of planes as flexibly as a single section. Attack
maneuvers now included vertical dives in section formation,
and we practiced tactical exercises of all kinds. Each day
brought a new and more interesting phase of training, until
we came at last to fixed gunnery, firing synchronized machine guns that shot between the blades of the whirling
propeller. This was fascinating work, diving on a sleeve target towed by another plane, placing the cross-hairs in our
telescope sights on the target, and squeezing the trigger on
the control stick to send a stream of bullets down at the
flying sleeve. I had trouble getting hits with fixed guns,
mainly because I couldn't believe it was necessary to lead
the target so far ahead with my telescope gun-sight. When
a target is flying by beneath you at more than a hundred
knots, you have to aim plenty of distance in front of it to
score any hits, as I found out by wasting a lot of ammunition.

Next came the phase of training which made a deeper
impression on me than anything I had ever experienced—
dive bombing. With half a dozen practice bombs in the racks
under our wings, we took off and climbed half a mile in the
air over a circular target marked out on the ground. One
at a time we peeled off from the formation and started down
in vertical dives, eyes glued on the target through the tele-

scope sights, engines roaring and wires screaming as the little thunderbirds neared terminal velocity. A quick jerk on the bomb-release toggle, then the steady, inexorable force of gravity pushing us down into the cockpit on the pull-out as we eased back to level flight. Then a glance backward to watch for the puff of white smoke from the exploding bomb, hoping to see it mushroom up inside of the target circle. That was dive bombing, the greatest thrill in aviation.

In this work we used the F4B-2's, which were ideal for this training because of their low terminal velocity. This gave us more time to square away in the dive and steady down with the telescope sight on the target. Contrary to a lot of wild hangar-flying theories we had heard, there was nothing uncomfortable about a properly executed bombing dive. "Going black" was unnecessary, and was the result of over-controlling or horsing back on the stick during the pull-out. Later on we were to practice dive bombing at terminal velocity in modern planes hour after hour with no bad after-effects.

Primary combat instruction followed—individual "dog-fights" with an instructor, who showed us all the tricks of the trade, getting above us with the sun at his back, or flying a tight flipper turn when we got on his tail until we tried to follow too closely and spun out of the turn. We were surprised to learn that dogfighting tactics have not changed since the first World War, and that any student who ignored the few elementary rules and tried anything fancy was immediately "shot down" by his instructor.

Before we realized it we were ready to leave the squadron and finish the course. I put in a request for duty with "any fighting squadron," and hoped for orders to the West Coast.

We had only one flight left—a night tactical exercise in division formation. That night when I drove over to the squadron, the field was strangely silent. Not a propeller was turning over on the airplanes lined up in front of the hangars. The students were standing around in small groups, talking in low voices. I went over to check out my parachute, but the enlisted man at the desk shook his head. "All flights are held up," he said slowly, "until they get the wreckage off the runway."

"What wreckage?" I asked, staring.

"One of the cadets just spun in, right on the north taxiway."

"Was he—hurt?"

"He was killed instantly."

All of us were shocked. It was hard to realize that Death had struck right in our midst, after nearly thirteen months of immunity. We were told that not one of us had to fly that night if we didn't want to—no false heroics about sending students out who had just been unnerved by the sudden death of a friend. But all of us chose to fly, mainly because the tragedy was still too close for us to feel it that night.

We were a sober-faced group when we lined up in our white uniforms the next morning to receive our wings and our orders to active duty. My assignment was to the dive bombers I had requested, in Fighting Squadron One, with orders to report to the USS Lexington at San Diego after a month's leave.

CHAPTER NINE

North Island

WITH A MONTH'S ADVANCE PAY IN MY POCKETS
and a bright new sword engraved with the Navy's insignia
in my luggage, I started for home. At first it was a relief
to get away from the routine I had been following for a year,
but after a couple of weeks I became strangely restless.
Civilian life was humdrum and colorless by comparison with
the stimulation and activity of the service. More than anything else, I missed the flying, so much so that by the end
of the third week it became an empty craving which had
to be satisfied. I drove out to the nearest airport, rented a
plane with the biggest engine I could find, and took off for
a half-hour flight that was like a cool drink of water to a
famished traveller. Flying was really in my system, and even
a hop in the little 90 H.P. sport plane was a refreshing experience after being on the ground for a few weeks.

Shipping my trunk by rail, I boarded an airliner in Chicago and settled back to relax while the states rolled by below. Twelve short hours later the big plane let down through the dusk over a golden sea of lights that stretched from one horizon to the other. From above, Los Angeles after dark was a sight so breath-taking that I could hardly believe it was real. No immigrant ever had a more inspiring first glimpse of a Promised Land than my first view of California and the West Coast from the air.

Staying overnight in Hollywood, I flew down to San Diego the next morning in an airliner that skirted the rocky range of mountains along the coast, with the blue Pacific off to the right. San Diego was bright, clear, and picturesque, but I hurried on across the bay to North Island, anxious to check in and get back to the Navy. North Island was almost deserted, and there was not an airplane in sight. When I reported to the Officer of the Day, I learned the reason. The squadrons had just embarked for a three weeks' cruise aboard the aircraft carriers. "You're the senior officer of your squadron in their absence," said the O.O.D. "Take charge and make yourself at home until your squadron returns."

This gave me a breathing spell to look around and become acclimated. In my squadron's hangar I found several spare airplanes, and was pleased to note that they were F4B-4's— later models of the same Boeing fighters I had flown at Pensacola. At least I would start out in a plane that was a little bit familiar to me. In an adjoining squadron I found an officer who had stayed behind to supervise some overhaul work, and bummed a ride with him in the rear cockpit of a scout-bomber, which gave me a chance to size up the landing area when it was not crowded.

Several other cadets checked in a few days later, and we all waited impatiently for the return of the squadrons. North Island was pleasant, with bright, warm days even in mid-November, and cool nights that called for blankets on our bunks. The cadet quarters were roomy and comfortable. We had our own mess, with colored mess attendants, and the food was excellent.

Finally the squadrons returned. We rushed out of the lounge at the first faint drone of the far-off propellers, and watched squadron after squadron, more planes than we had ever seen in the air at one time, approaching from the north, roaring past overhead, peeling off in beautifully timed break-ups for section landings.

That afternoon we checked in with the Squadron Duty Officer who introduced us to the Skipper, Lieutenant Commander G. A. Seitz, and the other squadron officers. There were twenty-two pilots in our squadron, including the eight aviation cadets, two of whom had arrived the month before, and seventy enlisted men. The latter did all the dirty work and deserve more credit than they ever receive. The squadron's enlisted machinists mates kept our planes and engines in perfect condition and the ordnancemen kept the machine guns and bomb-release mechanisms working, while the seamen did all of the manual labor and the yeomen handled the monotonous details of the office with its endless paper-work. All we had to do was assist the senior officers who supervised each division, such as gunnery, engineering, flight, or communications, and fly the airplanes. No finer, more capable group of men can be found in any work than the Navy enlisted men. In four years of flying with the Navy, I have never had an engine quit on me through any fault of the

enlisted men who overhauled it or the mechanic who kept
it in running order. Without perfect confidence in his airplane and its engine, no pilot is worth much to his squadron.
It is the men on the ground who really keep the planes in
the air.

As new pilots in the squadron, green and unfamiliar with
actual service operations, we were given a thorough indoc-
trination course that lasted several months. The Flight Officer, Lieutenant M. E. A. Gouin, was assigned the task of
working out a system of training for us that would enable
us to qualify as quickly as possible for a regular place in the
squadron formation. He trained us in section and division
tactics, showing us little tricks in bombing and gunnery that
enabled us to score more hits, patiently answering our in-
numerable questions, and slowly smoothing the rough edges
off our flying until we were qualified to fly with the squadron
as wingmen on the senior lieutenants who were section or
division leaders. All of us worked hard towards the day when
we could fly with "the Big Blue Team," or the regular pilots,
and graduate from "the Rinkeydinks," as they called the
group of supernumerary pilots who were still in a training
stage.

Lieutenant Gouin was the only pilot I ever saw who could
actually call his shots with fixed machine guns. He used to
draw a diagram for us on the blackboard, urging us to con-
centrate on a definite point of aim. "I will aim here," he
said, pointing to a spot on the target, "and my burst should
be right about there." At first we were inclined to be skep-
tical, until he took us out for a demonstration. When we
marked his first target, the individual holes of one burst were
so close together that I could stick my fist through the gap

in the cloth. His flying, bombing, and gunnery were inspiring to all of us, especially in view of his unassuming manner. I learned more real flying in those first few weeks in the squadron than I had in several months of student training.

The F4B-4's were a whole lot different from the light, fabric-covered F4B-1's and F4B-2's we had flown at Pensacola. These planes were all metal except the wing surfaces, and were loaded down with a lot of service equipment that included machine guns of .30 and .50 calibre, a life raft, emergency rations, flotation gear, a two-way radio, bomb-racks, belly tanks, and oxygen equipment. This added weight gave them entirely different handling characteristics, and we treated them with a great deal of respect, especially in the matter of cross-wind landings. A smoke-pot in the center of the South Field landing mat at North Island helped considerably at this stage of our training in giving us the true wind direction.

Several weeks after our arrival, the Landing Signal Officer of the USS Lexington flew down with us to Ream Field on the Mexican border, where he coached us for several days in the proper method of making an approach for a carrier landing. This approach technique, which I am not at liberty to describe here, required an entirely different kind of landing from any that we had made before. When the signal officer was satisfied with our performance, we returned to the squadron to await the arrival of the carrier.

The first time I ever saw an aircraft carrier, I had to go out and land my airplane on it. In this case it was the Saratoga, sister ship of the Lexington, which was in drydock. Lieutenant Gouin was on hand for a last word of reassuring advice when we took off, and as we circled North Island and climbed above Point Loma I saw the Saratoga, steaming majestically along with two plane-guard destroyers trailing in her wake, a dozen miles off the coast. In a few minutes we were circling over the ship, which in spite of its tremendous size looked all too small for a landing.

The weather was perfect and the Pacific as calm as a millpond. One after another, the planes ahead of me spiralled down for their landings and taxied up the deck. Soon it was my turn, and before I knew it I was starting my approach. Below me was the boiling wake of the big ship as she cruised ahead into the wind. Avoiding the foremast of the nearest destroyer, I steadied down on a straight course behind the carrier. As I sailed over the stern ramp I saw a broad grin on the face of the signal officer, just as he had looked during our practice landings on the field. I chopped the throttle, and the little plane settled down onto the deck in a landing as comfortable as I had ever made on the ground. There was a mild jerk as my tailhook engaged the arresting gear and came to an easy stop. A moment later I was taxying up the deck and preparing to take off for the next of the landings that would qualify me as a carrier pilot.

The whole program went off without a hitch. None of us had any trouble, and soon we were back aboard for a hearty meal in the Junior Officers' Mess. After lunch we wandered around the ship, marvelling at the unbelievable expanse of the hangar deck and the endless maze of passageways, wardrooms, galleys, and sleeping quarters. The officers' staterooms were as large and comfortable as any I had seen aboard the average ocean liner, adequately ventilated and equipped with innerspring mattresses. Everything aboard the ship was immaculate. The bright-work was polished until it glistened, all companionways and ladders were newly painted, and the teak flight deck was as clean as a kitchen table in a Dutch farmhouse.

That afternoon we took off for a rendezvous above the ship and a short flight back to North Island, elated with the prospect of the cruise we were soon to make on one of the finest ships in the world. So far, active duty had surpassed my fondest expectations. Life in the Navy was going to be all right.

CHAPTER TEN

Night Formation

OUR TRAINING CONTINUED, AND WE PRO-
gressed to night carrier landings, which were conducted on
a moonlit night when the Pacific was a molten silver sheet
and the dark bulk of the carrier was outlined in every detail
as we landed aboard. Night flying was a regular part of our
work. We held tactical maneuvers of some sort one night
each week until we felt as much at home in the air at night
as in the daytime. Then I had the closest call of my flying
career, an experience that shook my confidence and opened
my eyes to some of the risks that rode always along with us
like an invisible sword of Damocles above our heads.

With two other cadets, I was scheduled for a night formation flight to practice section tactics. We took off from North Island at dusk. Burke, in Number Seven, was leading the section, Dzendolet was on the left in Number Eight and I was on the right in Number Nine. Banking sharply to the left to avoid the three-hundred-foot ridge along Point Loma, we circled the field for altitude, waiting for a nasal voice to come through in the routine radio test: "Fighting One Group from Lexington Base: Test: Acknowledge." And one by one we answered: "Lexington Base from One Fox Seven, aye aye!" "Aye aye from One Fox Eight." "Nine, aye aye!"

This formality over, Burke led us down the Strand past Coronado to Border Field, circling over San Ysidro for a few moments to look at the garish neon lights of Tijuana across the Border, then heading east to Otay Mesa. Here he turned the lead over to Dzendolet, who led the way around between San Diego and the mountains to Camp Kearney, where Dzendolet turned the lead over to me. Over Camp Kearney, I broke up the section for the usual period of practice landings. Half an hour later I signaled for a rendezvous and turned the lead back to Burke, who headed for North Island.

The night was cool, but I had worn a heavy flying suit over my flight jacket and felt very comfortable. As we passed north of San Diego, I eased back a few yards to enjoy the brilliant pattern of the myriad twinkling lights below.

This was the way night flying should be, I told myself. Single-seaters were the only thing—nobody riding behind you to worry about in case of trouble—hop over the side if the engine quit, or even set 'em down on a strip of highway if the landing light wasn't on the blink. Flying these stubby fighters was a real treat, and I had never felt more comfortable while flying at night than I did then. The ship responded to the slightest touch of the controls or throttle, which helped ease the strain of the constant jockeying for position necessary in cruising along at a hundred knots only ten paces from the leader.

After we passed San Diego, Burke circled North Island and headed west. The air grew bumpy as we crossed over the Bay and I eased back a few yards, watching Burke's ship closely to avoid hitting it as he surged up and down in the rough air. The outline of Burke's ship grew dimmer as I increased my distance and step-up, so I shifted my gaze from the ship itself to the bright white gleam of the turtle-back light on the top of the fuselage. Out of the corner of my eye I saw the lights of the city crawl slowly past below me and disappear astern. Ahead and to the right were the lights of La Jolla, jutting out into the dark expanse of the Pacific.

The western sky had become overcast, merging with the sea to form a solid pall of inky blackness which obliterated all suggestion of a horizon. Against this formless background Burke's ship now seemed suspended in space. Every indication of motion was blotted out by the absence of anything above or below his ship which might indicate direction, speed or distance. Even the interval between the two planes seemed altered to some strange new dimension. When he decreased his speed with the throttle, his plane did not seem *closer*, but merely larger, and when he increased his speed, instead of seeming *farther* from me, it only seemed *smaller*. It was like the optical illusion of looking at one of those trick drawings which reverses itself after you stare at it for a few seconds.

I blinked my eyes, and the illusion disappeared, but in a few moments it returned. I blinked again, but it remained.

I shook my head, and again things were normal; distance was no longer size, but distance, as it should be.

Staring intently at the white light ahead of me, I concentrated on the task of keep the interval between the two ships from changing. This time I felt it with a distinct snap as the dimensions reversed themselves. Irritated, I jerked my head around and looked back over my right shoulder at the lights of the city behind me. Instantly my sense of orientation returned; my plane was no longer suspended in space, but moving forward.

Although my backward glance had been brief, I looked ahead again just in time to avoid hitting Burke's ship, which had been thrown up in front of me by a violent updraft. This would never do, I realized. Background or no background, I must keep my eyes where they belonged.

A quick glance over at Dzendolet's ship showed me that my own interval was too close, making an uneven formation. The second plane in the section always set the interval, so I obediently eased my throttle and dropped back a few yards until I was even with Dzendolet.

A few seconds later the other two ships seemed to be banking up in a right turn. I started to follow, but the controls felt queer. Glancing at the turn-and-bank indicator, I saw that the pointer indicated a *left* turn, while the ball showed a *right* bank. No help there, I thought; Burke must be skidding his turn.

An experienced pilot would have recognized the symptoms immediately. My plane was in a violent skid, diving to the left. I had the controls "crossed," and instead of trusting my instruments, I was trying to fly by the feel of the plane when there was no horizon for a reference point—a dangerous procedure which invariably results in a confused sense of equilibrium known to instructors as *vertigo*.

Soon it was apparent that I was falling behind the others, who now seemed to be above and ahead of me. I advanced my throttle, but the distance increased. In a moment I seemed to be in a vertical bank, but still they were pulling away from me.

Desperately I jammed on full gun, past the throttle-stop, in an effort to catch up. But still they pulled ahead of me. A glance at my airspeed indicator showed 130 knots, with the speed increasing. Still the inky blackness gave me no hint of my direction. The other two ships were now banked up vertically above me. My feeling of helplessness changed to resentment. What was Burke trying to do, a wing-over? Of all the crazy things to do at night! I reached for my microphone to protest.

Swiftly the other two ships drifted away and disappeared above me. A lone star appeared dead ahead over my engine cowling. Suddenly I felt a sickening, lost, suspended-in space sensation like that which preceeds a whip stall. My mind flashed ahead to the consequences: a vertical climb . . . the sudden loss of flying speed which would follow . . . the violent forward lurch of the plane from the weight of the heavy engine in its nose . . . the rending crunch as the engine snapped off its mountings . . .

Frantically I shoved the stick all the way forward in an attempt to recover from the stall, but instead of leveling off into normal flight, the ship behaved as if possessed; the controls stiffened, the wires screamed and the engine howled like a thousand devils. My goggles were snatched from my head as if by an unseen hand and the wind tore at my eyes.

I felt the safety belt dig into my thighs and the blood bulging the veins of my head, and knew that I had gone over on my back and that the ship was in inverted flight.

This was the first indication of my true predicament that I had had for several seconds. Fortunately the safety belt was fairly tight, and I could still reach the rudder pedals with my toes. Blinded by the terrific gale that beat into my eyes, I instinctively went through the motions of a half roll, easing the throttle back at the same time. The high-pitched scream of the wires gradually descended the scale, the gale died down and my sight returned enough for me to see a glow which marked an unnaturally high horizon.

Steadying down on this, I glanced at my instruments: airspeed 170 knots, altitude *200 feet*. Quickly I jerked the stick back and the black horizon dropped abruptly beneath me to reveal the lights of San Diego dead ahead. I had almost plowed straight into the ridge of Point Loma.

Only then, with the realization of the fate I had so narrowly escaped, did fear set in. I felt suddenly cold and weak. The thought of what had almost happened was repugnant, and in a few seconds it grew like an enormous, intangible thing of appalling proportions, as my mind tried to disbelieve it. My knees were shaking so hard that I could hardly keep my feet on the controls.

An insistent voice in my earphones recalled me: "One Fox Nine! One Fox Nine from One Fox Seven! Acknowledge!"

Mechanically I lifted the dangling microphone and forced myself to speak: "One Fox Seven from One Fox Nine. My goggles blew off. Am returning to base. Acknowledge."

My mind leaped to the new task. The lights of North Island were beneath me and my engine was purring along as smoothly as if nothing had ever happened. The whole incident seemed far away, impossible. I felt warm again, and my knees stopped shaking. Wiping my eyes with the back of my glove, I hunched forward to take advantage of the scanty protection offered by the wind-shield and scanned the horizon.

Far above me, the other two planes were circling the field together. Off to my right and below me, a division of Scouting Four was breaking up over the Strand. Violating all course rules, I cut in ahead of them and nosed down towards the flood light at the end of the landing mat. I nursed the ship along in a power glide, eased it down until the wheels touched, chopped the throttle back, and rolled to an easy stop. Then, after I was safely down, my knees began to shake again so violently that I could hardly taxi back to the hangar.

My mechanic stared at me curiously as I dragged myself out of the narrow cockpit. "Everything all right, sir?" he asked as he extended the inspection sheet for me to sign.

"Yes," I answered slowly, "everything's all right. But you very nearly lost your airplane tonight."

"How was that, sir?"

For a long moment I looked back over my shoulder at the black pall over Point Loma. "I don't know," I replied vaguely. "My goggles blew off." Absently I signed the inspection sheet and walked slowly away towards the squadron office. The ground felt strangely warm and comforting under my feet and the lights seemed unusually bright and pleasant.

A few minutes later the others hurried up. "What the devil happened to you?" demanded Burke. "Why did you run away from us?"

"Run away from *you?*" I cried angrily. "It's the other way

around! Why did you go into the wing-over? You nearly spun me in!"

"*What* wing-over? What are you talking about?"

"Don't try to give me that stuff! You know well enough. When we were headed west over Mission Beach. You went into a right wing-over, and I nearly did a whip stall trying to keep up with you. I damned near went in before I got straightened out."

"But we didn't turn right!" protested Burke. "We turned *left!*"

"Yeah," said Dzendolet, "and I looked out and saw you banked up on your side. You hung there a minute, then dived out under us like a flash. That was the last we saw of you until we heard you over the radio and saw you coming in to land."

I paled visibly. "Then you never turned to the right?"

"Of course not," said Burke. "I was about to bring us home, before you busted up the formation. We didn't know where the devil you had gone, till you finally answered after I had called you about five times."

"Then I was headed straight *down,* instead of up," I said, shuddering.

"What do you mean?" asked Dzendolet.

"I felt as if I was about to do a whip stall," I said. "So I pushed over, but instead of heading straight up, I must have been headed straight down. I thought I saw a star dead ahead, but it must have been a light on the beach."

"You mean you pushed over on your back from three thousand feet?" asked Burke incredulously.

"Yes," I answered faintly, "and with full gun."

"Great Fish!" said Dzendolet. "You did an outside loop!"

"Just half of one; I managed to roll out of it at the bottom."

"Well, if that's the case," drawled Burke, "from now on you're just living on borrowed time!"

"Fine damn thing!" said Dzendolet facetiously, "We'd never have found you. We'd have been out there all night dropping flares on the water."

"I guess you would. I must have had close to three hundred knots on the way down."

"How on earth did you ever get mixed up like that?" asked Burke.

"I don't know. I could have sworn you were turning the other way."

"It's easy to get confused on a dark night," said Dzendolet. "One night down at Pensacola we were flying cross-country formation to Mobile, and I got balled up as we crossed the bay. When we got there, I looked out and there was Mobile cocked up at a forty-five degree angle. 'Great Guns!' says I, 'is Mobile built on the side of a hill?' But it was me who was banked up on my side, as I found when I spun out of the formation."

"Yes, that's it; that's exactly what happened to me," I admitted.

We hung up our flight gear and started out into the night, walking along silently for a few moments. Suddenly I realized for the first time how closely I had come to having my life snuffed out like a dropped candle. I could almost see the others sorting out my jumbled personal effects to ship home. "By the way," I said absently, "the keys to my trunk are in the top drawer of my dresser. Don't bust it open."

"Say, what are you mumbling about?" asked Burke.

"Nothing," I said, snapping back with a start. "Let's eat."

CHAPTER ELEVEN

The Spring Cruise

A FEW WEEKS LATER OUR TRAINING WAS COM-
plete, and I was assigned a plane of my own and a place in
the squadron's regular tactical organization as a wingman
in the second section. Then we began our preparations for
the annual fleet maneuvers, which were to be held between
the Hawaiian Islands and Midway Island. Packing all our
personal gear for a two-month stay aboard ship, we sent
our luggage to be ferried out on a lighter to the Lexington,
which lay at anchor off Coronado Roads. When the crew
was embarked, the carrier weighed anchor, and as soon as
she was underway the squadrons took off from North Island
and landed aboard.

For the first few days we plowed through heavy weather

that kept half of the new pilots in their bunks, for although the Lexington held the world's speed record for the longest 24-hour run, we crept along with the slower ships of the train, rolling and pitching through towering seas piled up by a hard blow. At last the weather cleared, and we were able to go topside and look around. We found ourselves in the center of the Pacific Fleet. All around us were ships, as far as the eye could reach—destroyers, light cruisers, supply ships, heavy cruisers, the giant battlewagons, and three other aircraft carriers. At night the twinkling lights could easily have been mistaken for those of a fair-sized city, transplanted hundreds of miles out to sea.

After a couple of weeks aboard ship, we had been lounging around the wardroom, smoking, reading and playing acey-deucy or cribbage, until we had begun to think that with an hour's formation tactics and a refresher landing every other day or so, the War Problem was going to be pretty soft. The Spring Cruise had become just a pleasant vacation from the usual routine of gunnery and dive-bombing.

And then one night we were awakened by the sound of a loud gong and a strident bugle call over the annunciator, followed by the whistle of a bo's'n's pipe and the ominous command: "Man all Flight Quarter Stations! Man all Flight Deck Fire Stations! Man all Torpedo Defense Stations!"

The "War" was on! I snapped on the light at the head of my bunk and looked at my watch. Three thirty a.m. Whew! No wonder I felt sleepy! Pulling on my clothes, I grabbed my flight gear, groped my way along shadowy passageways dimly illuminated by the weird blue glow of the battle lights, and climbed the ladder into the armored ready-room on the flight deck. A yeoman was chalking up data concerning our mission and objective on a blackboard, and we hurriedly copied this vital information onto the blank columns of our navigation boards, checking the figures carefully, for upon their accuracy would depend our safe return to the carrier. Latitude: far enough south to see the Southern Cross; longitude: near the 180th meridian, where the calendar gets all mixed up; nearest land: *out of range,* or, as some wag grimly put it, two miles away—straight down. We copied down the carrier's speed and probable course after launching, and noted that the magnetic compass variation had changed five degrees since we embarked.

Our squadron's task was to act as a high outer patrol, ahead of the destroyer screen which spread out fanwise in front of the advancing fleet. The destroyers, or "Brides of Death," were on the lookout for "enemy" submarines, but they were also ready to rush in as soon as the enemy fleet was sighted, running the gantlet of fire from the cruisers in an attempt to deliver their deadly broadside of torpedoes at the big battleships in the enemy's main battle line. Our own battle line was similarly protected by a line of heavy cruisers and an outer line of light cruisers. All of these larger ships carried observation seaplanes ready to be catapulted as soon as the enemy fleet was within range, to spot the salvoes fired by the long range guns.

High above and in advance of our own fleet, we would be in a position to pounce upon any enemy aircraft or submarines that might be sighted. We knew that their submarines would probably be lying in wait across our own fleet's path, submerged with their engines silenced so that our destroyers could not hear them with listening devices, ready to emerge as soon as our cruisers had passed over them and torpedo our battleships or carriers from close range. From this position we could also parry or harass any attacks made by the enemy aircraft squadrons, whether it was a swift thrust of their torpedo planes flying just above the surface of the water, or an attack from above by a squadron of fighters or heavy dive bombers. The big patrol bombers might attack from any altitude, dropping torpedoes at sea level, or using horizontal bombing technique from high altitudes. Our surface ships might be the first to sight the enemy, in which case they would warn us by radio and direct us to the attack.

The aircraft carriers, the cruisers, destroyers, and submarines might help to shift the advantage in the coming sea battle; aircraft superiority might be the decisive factor. But the main event, we knew, would be fought out by the big battlewagons, pounding away at each other with their big guns as soon as they were within firing range, even though they might be out of each other's sight beyond the horizon. In which case, our planes would be the eyes of the fleet.

From outside came the grinding squeal of a hundred inertia starters, followed by a muffled roar as all of the engines were started in unison at a signal from the bridge. Then came the command: "Pilots, man your planes!"

Grabbing a wad of cotton from the bulkhead container, I stuffed it into my ears and stepped out into the night. A gale that nearly knocked me down was blowing along the flight deck, augmented by the propeller blasts of planes packed so closely together that there was no room to walk between them. Ghostly blue flames from the exhaust stacks outlined the engines, giving enough light for me to crawl on all fours under the wings and fuselages towards the area designated for our squadron. My progress was slow and cautious, for I knew that one false move would let the gale drag me to sudden death in a churning propeller.

Feeling my way along, I crept under a squadron of scouts, wriggled through a squadron of bombers and eventually reached the first of the group of stubby fighters. Finally, after what seemed like miles, I reached my plane. My mechanic hung onto a strut to brace himself against the wind as he helped me into the narrow cockpit.

Lights were forbidden, so I carefully checked my engine by the phosphorescent glow of the dials on the instruments or by sense of touch, testing the magneto on each switch, feeling for the indicator on the stabilizer control, pulling back the mixture control until I was sure that it was on full rich for the take-off, shifting my prop into low pitch, and switching the gasoline valve to the main tank. Finally I signed the inspection sheet, indicating that I accepted the plane for flight, and held the brake-pedals down while the mechanic removed the chocks, with plenty of throttle on to keep from being blown back into the propeller of the plane behind me.

One by one the planes ahead taxied up the deck and disappeared. Then a dim light rotating in the hand of a mechanic signaled me to taxi ahead. Soon I was alone at the front of the line. I released my brakes and started to roll ahead, fighting the air currents which tried to skid me over the side before my plane had attained flying speed. The plane bumped along the deck, logy with the full gasoline load, and finally staggered off into the air. A moment later I had full control, and nosed up towards the line of faint lights which glowed from the tails of the other planes in my squadron. I flew with the stick between my knees while I struggled into my parachute harness. Switching the gasoline valve to the belly-tank, I leaned out the mixture to conserve fuel for the long hours ahead.

The horizon was beginning to glow with approaching dawn, and as the squadron climbed up through the scattered clouds, the sky brightened rapidly until the sun burst above the rim of the horizon with a ruddy glare. Far below, I could barely make out the wake of the carrier, a dim white streak on the gloomy expanse of a darkened world.

My plane was number three of the second section. The Skipper, leading the group in a V of V's, was keeping the formation closed up so that he could shift at once into attacking disposition if the "enemy" was sighted. He climbed steadily until the 12,000 foot level was reached and the temperature dropped until I glanced at my strut thermometer apprehensively. Five degrees below zero, Centigrade. I turned on more carburetor heat, to keep the jets from icing up, and pulled the collar of my flying suit up around my neck.

My radio began to pick up engine static, but I could not reduce the volume without taking a chance of missing the all-important contact reports. Glancing at my instruments, I noticed that the oil temperature was approaching the danger line. I tried a richer gasoline mixture, even though it wasted precious fuel, for a forced landing would necessitate breaking radio silence and disclosing our position to the enemy radio operators who were maintaining a continuous vigil with their direction finders. The noise in my earphones increased until my brain throbbed painfully, forcing me to reduce the volume. Catching my section leader's eye, I pointed to my earphones and shook my head. He nodded, understanding that my radio was out of commission.

An hour dragged by and I became so cold that my teeth chattered and my flying became ragged from shivering. The section leader signaled that he had a radio message and after he decoded it I flew close above him while he laboriously relayed it to me in visual Morse code, by tapping his hand up and down on the edge of the wind-shield: "Carrier changed course at 0547 to 165 degrees speed 26 knots."

Fumbling for a pencil with numbed fingers, I worked out the problem on my navigation board, keeping one eye on the other planes in the formation and one hand on the throttle as I flew with the stick between my knees. The skipper increased his speed and when I put on more engine revolutions to catch up, the noise in my earphones died down somewhat.

My arm began to ache from the continuous strain of holding the left wing up; that last hard carrier landing must have thrown the rigging slightly out of alignment. I was forced to use more right rudder than usual, and my leg grew numb from the awkward position. When I attempted to relax by taking my right foot off the rudder pedal, the ship yawed so violently that I had to bank steeply to keep from hitting the other wing man. He was so close that I could see the startled look on his face.

The cold was so intense in the open cockpit that I was shaking all over. I looked down at the Skipper and decided that he must have ice in his veins to be able to sit there without showing that he felt it. Violent cramps seized my right leg and the pain was so great that I was afraid I would have to drop out of formation. I cursed the day airplanes were invented. Never in my life had I been so uncomfortable. Just when I felt that I could stand it no longer and began

to fear that I would have to spoil the entire war problem
by an emergency landing, a voice booming over the radio
nearly knocked off my earphones: "Attack enemy patrol
plane bearing three forty, course ninety, altitude 1000 feet!"

There was no mistaking the voice or the volume. That was
our carrier relaying a message flashed to it by one of the
other ships. The skipper signaled to my section leader to
break off and I followed him to the attack. Nosing over
steeply, he plunged down at 150 . . . 200 . . . 250 knots, until
the speed of the dive forced me to stand on the left rudder
pedal and the cramps in my leg disappeared.

The section plunged through a hole in the clouds and
eased out at the two-thousand-foot level, roaring along at full
gun towards the area where the carrier had reported the
enemy plane. A minute later we spotted it and climbed
towards the base of the clouds for the attack. The section
leader led the way, starting his dive out of the sun. Number
Two followed and I went down close on his tail, watching
the size of the target through my telescope sight. As we
approached within range, I pressed the camera gun trigger,
following through for an instant and easing out of the dive
I caught a glimpse of the machine gunners following me
with their sights as I swished past the big boat, and made a
mental note of the squadron number for my contact report.

A moment later, my engine sputtered and missed fire. Instantly I leaned out my mixture control, but still my plane
headed for the water. Then I remembered my gasoline valve
and switched it back to the main tank. In my excitement I
had entered a dive with the auxiliary gas supply consumed.
A few strokes on the hand wobble-pump restored fuel pressure and the engine perked along smoothly again.

The section leader pointed his plane's nose towards the clouds to rejoin the rest of the squadron above. A few minutes more and we were again undergoing the tortures of the damned. A relief was afforded when the squadron was directed to bomb three attacking enemy cruisers.

This time we climbed up over the condensation layer to take advantage of the protecting cover of a layer of scattered clouds at the 12,000-foot level. Maneuvering the squadron until we had the sun behind us, the Skipper shifted us into open formation and rocked his wings to signal for an attack.

One by one the planes ahead of me followed swiftly, nosing over in a vertical dive through a hole in the clouds, slanting down along the sun-lane which would blind the enemy anti-aircraft gunners. As I dived at one of the big warships, lining up the cross-hairs in my telescope sight on the machine-gun nests in her fighting tops, I wondered how many of us would be able to pull out of such a dive if we were playing for keeps. In war time those flashes from her searchlights, simulating anti-aircraft fire, would be throwing live shells up at us as fast as our machine-gun bullets and bombs rained down at her. Who would be able to get in the most hits first? Would anybody live to tell the tale?

Zooming back heavenward on the momentum of the dive, we climbed at full throttle to regain the protection of the clouds before the cruisers could radio for the assistance of their own carrier squadrons.

No sooner was this mission completed than another message came over the radio: "Urgent! Enemy submarine five hundred yards off the starboard bow!" Again our section was designated by the Skipper to make the attack. It was some time before we located the submarine, a sinister shadow among the shadows of clouds, marked only by the thin wake of the periscope, which could hardly be distinguished from the whitecaps around it.

Swooping low over the water, I removed a bomb-shaped smoke flare from its holder over the .50-calibre machine gun, and flung it down past my stabilizer into the path of the submerged raider. The other two planes did likewise and soon three plumes of smoke on the water around the submarine indicated to the observers that it had been bombed. The section leader signaled for me to rejoin him and as I zoomed up I wondered whether we "sank" the sub before it had time to put our carrier out of action with simulated torpedo fire.

The carrier signaled for all squadrons to return. Soon they were sweeping around the ship in a wide circle, each awaiting its turn to land. Three other squadrons had to land aboard before it was our turn, and I fidgeted and squirmed around in the cockpit trying to get a more comfortable position on the hard parachute pack for the long wait. A squadron of our own scout-bombers, returning from an attack on the enemy fleet, cut across our path, and I fought to control my little ship as it was tossed around like a leaf in the slip streams from a dozen ten-foot propellers.

Finally the other squadrons were aboard, and again there was the struggle to unbuckle my parachute while both hands were busy trying to keep position in a banking, spiralling formation. One after another the planes ahead of me landed aboard, and I started to make my approach. But just as I was about to cut my gun and drop onto the pitching deck, the signal officer frantically waved me off. Jamming on full gun, I pulled out to the left to miss the carrier's stacks. The carrier had been slightly out of the wind, and my plane had been drawn into the stack-wash—turbulent air currents which might have spun me in.

Taking a deep breath and a firm grip on the stick, I started my approach again. The stern of the carrier rose and fell threateningly and I forced myself to hold my course, fighting off the instinct to pour on the coal and pull up out of danger. A moment later I chopped my throttle and nosed over quickly to follow the receding deck. There was a bounce, a jolt, and I was safely aboard. Quickly I taxied forward to make room for the next plane to land behind me.

Then I dragged myself out of the cockpit and limped stiffly along the deck towards the officer's mess, glad that it was all over and that I could quiet my crawling stomach with some hot breakfast. Lighting a much-needed cigarette, I ordered enough food for three ordinary persons and leaned back to relax.

Suddenly I heard the anti-aircraft batteries on the gun galleries popping away with their blank loads, followed by the snarling roar of planes pulling out of a dive-bombing attack over the ship. The alarm gong clanged, and I grabbed my flight gear and hurried back up to the ready-room.

"Who is it?" I asked, peering through a port-hole at the *melee* of planes milling around over the ship.

"The Ranger gang!" someone answered. "We've got to get off and follow them back!"

Again the command boomed over the annunciator: "All pilots man planes!"

Wearily I dragged myself up and into the cockpit, resigned to a repetition of the gruelling hours I had just endured. I began to wonder if it was all worth the effort.

But a week later, when the first part of the problem was finished and we were relaxing under the palm trees on a hotel terrace with cool drinks in our hands and soft Hawaiian music in our ears, I knew the answer. At the table next to me, my wing-mate sat talking to an attractive girl, who looked up into his eyes and said, "Tell me, is it really fun, this flying for the Navy?"

He gazed out for a moment across the blue water before replying. I could almost read his thoughts as he remembered the highlights of the action and forgot the cold, the fatigue, and the discomfort. He turned to her with a smile. "It sure is, Honey," he answered fervently. "It's more fun than anything else in the whole wide world!"

CHAPTER TWELVE

Wheels over Water

AT THE CONCLUSION OF THE FIRST PART OF the maneuvers, the Fleet anchored off Diamond Head on the Island of Oahu. Off to the left lay Pearl Harbor and the city of Honolulu. A layer of clouds wreathed the mountainous dome of the island down to the sugar-cane and pineapple plantations above the city. The Hawaiian Islands, jutting abruptly out of a boundless ocean, looked unreal in their bright green beauty, like enchanted islands from some mediaeval fairy tale. None of the advance publicity I had read could possibly do justice to the real thing. Here was one garden spot of the world which the press agents had not over-rated.

Shore leave—fishing, trying the surf boards in Waikiki Beach's rolling combers, cocktail parties, dances, and banquets—this was like heaven itself after three weeks at sea. We shopped in the oriental stores, tried Japanese *sake* and exotic Chinese foods, admired the graceful Hawaiian hula dancers, and forgot all our troubles in ten glorious days ashore. Then *aloha* to the Happy Isles, and back to sea for the serious business of war exercises.

Cruising eastward, we saw the islands sink down below the western horizon. The Lexington veered off to the northeast, temporarily leaving the rest of the fleet. The next day we were in the air at dawn, out again on a tactical exercise that carried us a hundred miles away from the ship. Hours later, but somewhat earlier than usual, a general recall of all squadrons came over the radio. The exercises were cut short as we headed south to intercept the carrier. Half an hour later we sighted her.

As we approached the carrier for the rendezvous of squadrons, a second radio message gave us the order of landings. The other squadron of fighters was to land first, the scouting squadron second, our squadron third, followed by the light bombers, with the heavy bombers last. Our Skipper acknowledged over the voice radio, and I settled back in the cockpit for a long wait. More than fifty other planes had to be taken aboard before it was my turn.

The first squadron spiraled down to the landing circle while the remaining four squadrons cruised in wide circles above the carrier. I checked my instrument readings and tried to estimate how long it would be before I could get a cigarette and a cup of coffee. Half an hour, maybe, at the most. The minutes dragged by, and I glanced idly at the ship to see how many planes had landed. There were only three aboard, and as I watched another plane making its approach, it veered off and circled around for another try. The ship seemed to be rolling heavily, which accounted for the delay.

Studying the wave pattern for a moment, I saw the cause. The long swells piled up by the prevailing Northeast Trades were now scarred by a cross-chop from a southeast wind that had come up within the last hour, so that the carrier, which had to head directly into the wind before she could take us aboard, was getting the bigger waves almost broad on her port beam. This sudden shift of the prevailing wind could mean only one thing: bad weather in our vicinity. A clicking of static in my earphones grew louder.

Scanning the horizon, I saw that the disturbance was closer than I had realized. A long line of white clouds was off to the south, their tops gleaming in the noonday sun. The ship was headed towards the cloud front at an angle of about forty-five degrees, and the distance was closing so rapidly that by the time the second squadron had entered the landing circle it was apparent that some of us were going to be caught short. Although the cloud bank was not more than ten thousand feet high, it covered a much greater area than I had expected. We could easily have flown over it, but it was soon evident that we would not be able to fly around it.

As the ominous wall approached, I saw that there was a dense curtain of rain streaming down from its lower edge. In addition to bad wind conditions, we were going to have poor visibility if we had to follow the carrier into the bad weather.

The carrier plowed straight ahead into the wind, rolling and pitching as she struck the swells. From our altitude it was difficult to realize how rough a sea she was bucking until a cloud of spray shot over the forward end of the flight deck, which had been high and dry above the roughest weather we had seen during the previous six weeks of the cruise. No wonder the boys were having a tough time getting aboard!

Easing my plane back a few yards to avoid running into my section leader's plane, I watched the race against time which was taking place below us. As fast as one plane managed to get aboard, another broke off from the section above to take its place in the landing circle, while from the level above, another three-plane section broke off from the squadron and spiraled down to await its progressive turn in the procession. Five squadrons of high-speed war planes circling around an airport a hundred yards long and twenty yards wide—a rolling, pitching platform moving ahead into a rainstorm that was bearing down on it at twenty or thirty miles an hour. There was a rhythm about the whole procedure that was fascinating in that it could not be hurried; any departure from the elementary rules of timing involved, and chaos would have been the result. The geometric precision of the procedure would have been upset, the pattern of circles and spirals would overlap, confusion would supplant order, and disaster would be the inevitable penalty. At last I realized what "air discipline" really meant. No hurry, no panic, no confusion—just the same timing and coordination, under pressure, that would exist under ideal conditions.

The cloud front was just ahead of the carrier now, with only half of the second squadron safely aboard. The curtain of rain streaming down from our level seemed as dense as a solid wall. It advanced swiftly on the ship, absorbed her bow, enveloped her superstructure, and obliterated her completely. She was gone like a ghost into a shadow.

The squadron ahead of us closed up to a tight formation and vanished into the wall of rain. My section leader waved his flippers as a sign to close up, as he moved down just above and to one side of the section ahead of him. I tensed up a bit more as I realized that we were about to follow the carrier into the bad weather. From bright sunlight we entered the dark shadow of the towering clouds, a momentary warning before we plunged into the grey wall that rushed headlong to meet us. The rain hit suddenly, stinging my forehead above my goggles. I withdrew my head below the edge of the stubby windshield, which deflected the blast up and over the open cockpit. The rain streaked by in horizontal white lines. Dimly I could make out the dark shadow of my section leader's plane, although my wingman, only a few feet farther away, was invisible. For all I knew, he might have pulled out of the formation, yet I felt that he must be there, flying wing and tail on our section leader, just as I was doing. And our section leader, I knew, was just as busy as I was, trying to keep the last wingman of the section below him in sight. The whole squadron was held together in the same manner, each pilot trusting the man ahead of him, with the Skipper flying by his instruments at the head of the procession. And somewhere in that blinding white stream were two other squadrons, linked by similar invisible ties, all relying on their skippers to take them through to safety.

A few minutes of this, and then I noticed a tendency to skid slightly to one side. A quick glance at my turn-and-bank indicator showed the pointer over to the left: either my section leader was pulling out of the formation, or the Skipper was making a turn to lead the squadron back into the clear weather. If the former was the case, we were in a tight spot, for if the squadron ever split up into sections, or if individual planes became separated and started milling around in that

blinding deluge, someone was going to be hit. I fought off
a wild desire to pull up and out of all this uncertainty, but
soon the turn-and-bank pointer swung back to the center of
the dial and the compass steadied down on a north course.
The Skipper was leading us out of it.

The parallel white streaks of rain assumed a bluish tinge.
The outlines of my section leader's plane became more distinct, and suddenly we burst out into the clear. A quick
glance around showed that the squadron was still intact—
eighteen planes still following the leader, with no one pulling
out in a pinch—another score for air discipline. The Skipper
swung us around in a wide circle to the right, until we
headed eastward along the cloud front. As I glanced at the
wall of rain the squadron of heavy bombers erupted from it
like a string of darts from some gigantic crossbow—all intact
and in proper formation. They fell in behind us.

The minutes crawled by as we flew along the cloud front
which stretched interminably to the east. At first I hoped
that we might be able to fly around it, but the cloud mass
became thicker, covering the horizon as far as the eye could
see. I glanced at my fuel gauge. There was gasoline for per-
haps another hour, no more. After that, a water landing, on
wheels built for good solid ground or a hard wooden deck.
Well, maybe I could set her down so she would float for a
while, I told myself.

But one look at the angry sea below us was enough to
wash that idea out of my mind. The waves were twenty or
thirty feet high, with a nasty cross-chop that would make any
attempt at a timed landing impossible. And to fly into a solid
wall of water at sixty or seventy knots would shred into
splinters any airplane ever built. Frantically my mind leaped

back to the land—there *must* be land somewhere that we could reach. But even before I looked at the data on my chartboard, I knew the answer: "Nearest land: out of range."

With this realization the minutes which had been crawling now raced by. One hour to go, and then . . . This must be how it would be in war time, I reflected. After the carrier had been bombed or torpedoed and we had no place to go—no place but the water. A landplane with wheels, and nothing to land on. Well, at least it would be quick!

Staring across at my wingman, I noticed that his face was tense and set. My expression must have been just as tense, for when he caught my eye he grinned. I raised my eyebrows questioningly, and he pointed his hand to indicate a long dive, and then held his nose like a small boy jumping off a springboard. The pantomime was so vivid it came like a cold shock to see my own thoughts reflected by his. Then he shook his head and smiled as though laughing to himself. For the life of me I could not see why. I knew he had a wife and two children back home, and how he could find humor in the situation was beyond me.

Then the utter incongruity of the situation struck me. Here we were, sailing smoothly along in bright sunshine, with comfort and safety just out of reach behind an overgrown rain-squall, flying the most advanced product of modern machinery, helplessly watching our engines run down like unwound clocks. Three whole squadrons of airplanes about to go down at sea. It was fantastic. Fair weather one minute, storm the next, depending on whether we flew south or east. And nothing to do but sit and take it.

My mind grasped at non-essentials—the letter I had neglected to write home from our last port, and the distant cousin I was supposed to look up when we got back to San Francisco. When we got back—*that* was it!

The carrier's radio booming in my ears snapped me back to strained attention: "Fightron One! Bombron Five! Bombron Six, from Lexington! We have reached clear weather only a few miles south. Proceed through bad weather area until you sight us. Acknowledge!"

"Com Fightron One, Aye, aye!" answered our Skipper's voice, followed immediately by acknowledgements from the other two squadron commanders.

Again we headed south towards the cloud front, closing up to a tight formation in order to maintain sight contact. Once more the stinging rain tore at our faces, but this time we disregarded it, for clear weather and safety were only a few miles ahead. Gradually the driving rain thinned out. We had glimpses of low, scudding clouds, then burst into the clear.

Ahead of us lay the carrier, in a natural amphitheatre of bright sunshine that glistened on her wet deck. There were dark clouds behind us and on both sides, but to the southeast the sky was blue and an open pathway stretched on out to the horizon. The ship was barely making headway as she wallowed through the troughs of the giant swells stirred up by the disturbance she had just passed through. One or two planes of the scouting squadron were still in the lower landing circle; the rest were safely aboard.

By the time we were in position over the ship it was our turn, and our skipper broke off the first section without delay. The first two planes managed to get aboard, but the third was waved off when the stern of the deck dropped out from under him just as he was about to land, and he had to go around again for another try. I glanced apprehensively at my fuel gauge. Every minute counted now. With relief I found that I still had enough fuel for half an hour. The bombing squadrons circling above us had bigger fuel tanks, with a proportionately longer flying range.

At last the first section was aboard, and it was our turn to go down. My section leader signaled for a right echelon, and my wingman slid over to his position behind me. Not until we spiraled down close to the water did I realize how much the ship was rolling and pitching. I had never seen her tossed around like this before.

Quickly I ran through my check-off list: landing hook down, mixture control rich, prop in low pitch, carburetor heat off, seat up, 'chute off. I struggled out of my parachute harness, for the heavy pack would have dragged me down like an anchor if I skidded off that wet deck and dropped over the side, even if I managed to struggle clear of the plane.

Watching my section leader's approach carefully, I tried to time my arrival so that I would be coming aboard just as soon as he was clear of the landing area. Two thousand men aboard that ship were concentrating on each landing, trying to get us all aboard before our fuel tanks ran dry. Every second was important, for one bungled approach might mean that someone would go down at sea.

The plane ahead of me was almost up to the ship. I saw the stern ramp rise yards above it, then drop far below. A moment later the plane was down, but instantly there was a blast of white steam from the ship's stacks—the signal for a deck crash. I pulled up and out to one side. As I flew past I could see the deck crew rushing for the stricken airplane. It lay motionless at a grotesque angle with the deck. Luckily there was no fire.

Circling again for another approach, I was again warned away. As I passed above the deck again I could see the crash crew walking the smashed plane up the deck, like ants around the body of a dead wasp. A weak feeling seized the pit of my stomach. I wondered about the fate of the pilot. Was he . . . ? But there was no time for idle speculation, for *my turn was next.*

This time the deck was clear, and I concentrated on the approach. At first I was high, then I over-corrected and approached too low—a sure form of suicide. A little more throttle, and I was back up in proper position. Now I was over the stern, which was luckily level for a moment. Chopping the throttle off, I held my breath and eased the stick back. There was a jolt as the wheels struck the deck, a jerk as the landing hook engaged the arresting gear, and I was safely aboard. The plane spotters waved me ahead. Split seconds behind me my wingman was trying to land. Shoving the throttle forward, I blasted the plane into motion and taxied up the deck out of his way. I cut the switch, and the propeller kicked over and stopped.

At last I could relax. I exhaled slowly, and then the reaction set in. My knees began to shake so that I could hardly keep my feet on the brake pedals while the mechanics put chocks under the wheels.

Finally I climbed weakly out of the cockpit, and then had a real thrill when I saw my section leader, safe and sound, busily inspecting his plane's wrecked under-carriage.

The snarl of a propeller overhead drew all eyes upward. Someone else had to go around again. "Come on!" cried my wingman, climbing down from his plane. "Let's go back and watch the others come aboard!"

Together we hurried back along the slippery deck and clambered up on top of the after gun turret, which gave us a grandstand view of the performance. We were no sooner there than we saw another crack-up. The ship rolled heavily as one of the larger bombers taxied up the wet deck, and the big plane slid sidewise. It smashed into the turret on which we were standing, badly damaging the plane. The pilot climbed out unscratched.

Half a dozen other planes managed to get aboard safely, then the ship struck a huge swell that made her stern pitch high in the air just as one of the bombers leveled off for a landing. The pilot nosed over in a frantic attempt to get down, and the plane's wheels hit the deck with terrific force. With a tremendous bounce, the big plane sailed past our turret like some monstrous insect, then squashed down into the mass of parked planes beyond. There was a confused jumble of men and airplanes, sirens and whistles, but the after part of the deck was clear and the remaining planes continued to come aboard with machine-like precision.

Ten minutes later it was all over. We could hardly believe that every plane had been brought back aboard the carrier under almost impossible conditions. Five planes were badly damaged, two of them wrecked beyond repair, *but not a single man had been injured.*

That night as we relaxed in the comfort and security of the wardroom after a hearty meal, the operations plan for the next day was announced. The maneuvers were to continue where we had left off that day. First call would be at three forty-five in the morning, for the squadrons would take off again at dawn.

CHAPTER THIRTEEN

Live Load

A WEEK LATER WE CAUGHT THE UNMISTAK-
able, fresh, pungent odor of the land, invisible behind a fog-
bank off California's rocky coast. The next day the fog lifted,
and all of the squadrons took off for a gigantic aerial parade
over San Francisco to dedicate the newly completed Golden
Gate Bridge. On our return to the ship we had to land
aboard under unfavorable conditions. The flight deck of the
carrier was rolling nearly thirty degrees, and the stern ramp
was pitching nearly fifty feet at times. Several planes were
badly damaged coming aboard, but again Death took a
holiday, and there were not even any injuries.

Anchoring in San Francisco Bay, we went ashore for a
week of royal welcome, then steamed out through the Golden
Gate to head for North Island. When we flew our planes
ashore, it seemed strange to set them down again on *terra
firma*, after nothing but carrier landings for nearly two
months. Most of us avoided the landing mat and used the

grassy edge of the field for our landings, to avoid ground-looping or leveling off too high, but even with these precautions there were some pretty fancy landings. All of the married officers' wives were waiting in front of the hangar, and it was a real homecoming.

The subsequent weeks saw the squadron routine resumed. Gunnery drill brought new and interesting exercises, including an experimental long range fixed-gun practice that increased my respect for the accuracy of synchronized machine guns. Dive bombing followed, but this time we started our approaches from fifteen thousand feet, reaching terminal velocity in every dive.

Then the Skipper announced that we were to take part in a live load practice in which we would use real bombs. Several days were devoted to preparing for this practice, and just before the take-off the squadron gunnery officer gave us a final lecture on safety precautions. "And don't forget to arm your bombs," he told us as he wound up his talk before the assembled pilots of the squadron. "We've all been dropping practice bombs for so long it will be hard to get used to live ones. If you drop these bombs unarmed they won't explode, and you'll bring the squadron's score down. Any questions?" he asked with a pause. "All right; go get some hits."

We filed out of the squadron office towards our planes, which were waiting with their engines turning up, and prepared to take off from the field. I climbed into the narrow cockpit of my plane, opened the throttle momentarily to test the magnetoes, and taxied out behind my section leader. There was hardly a breath of wind; the smoke from the smudge-pot in the center of the landing mat was rising almost straight up in the still air.

The Skipper's section preceded us, and after a long run across the field we were off. As we rose above the ridge of Point Loma I noticed that the mountains east of us were standing out with crystal clarity; it was one of those rare days when the visibility was almost perfect. We could see for miles. I stole a quick glance out to the right, taking my eyes off my section leader's plane for a moment, and saw the carrier, steaming along ten or twelve miles off the coast, looking like a miniature ship set on a table mirror. The two plane-guard destroyers trailing along in her wake looked like dories at that distance, but the carrier's wake was visible for miles behind her in the glassy water. Today the Pacific was really living up to its name.

As soon as the squadron rendezvous had been effected, the Skipper headed out to sea, and in a short time we were circling over the carrier. The landings proceeded like clockwork; not one pilot ahead of me was given a wave-off, and as I approached for my landing I was unable to detect any roll or pitch of the carrier's deck. For once, at least, conditions for carrier operations were perfect.

This time I felt perfectly at ease as I brought my plane in for a landing. There was hardly a jolt as the wheels touched the deck, and the usual jerk as the landing hook engaged the arresting gear was almost imperceptible. I taxied on up the deck and was spotted well forward. The landings continued uneventfully until all squadrons were aboard. There was not even a blown-out tire to mar the procedure.

And now the real business of the day was at hand. From the magazines deep in the bowels of the ship, the bombs and machine-gun ammunition were brought up to the flight deck. In spite of myself, I felt my heart beat a little faster as I saw

the first of the bombs, long, streamlined, sinister objects that
looked much more efficient than the clumsy tin, water-filled
substitutes we had been dropping in practice. These really
looked as though they meant business. And when I reflected
that each one carried a hundred pounds of TNT in a steel
case whose fragments could clean off the whole end of the
flight deck, my respect for them increased even more.

Then two ordnancemen passed by me, trundling one of the
500-pounders aft for one of the scout-bombers. My eyes
widened as I watched it, but a moment later I stared open-
mouthed at a tremendous cylinder with stubby fins, so big it
took four men to handle it—a thousand-pound demolition
bomb for one of the heavy bombers. Compared with that
monster, my two little hundred-pound fragmentation bombs
looked like sweet potatoes.

What if one of those should go off . . . my mind could not
even picture the consequences. But when I saw the nonchal-
ance with which the ordnancemen handled their deadly
charges, I absorbed some of their confidence, and soon became engrossed in checking the loading process.

This was to be a genuine rehearsal, with a full load of
fuel and machine-gun ammunition to simulate actual war-
time conditions. Off to the south there was a tug towing a
barge which was to serve as a target. We were to take off
from the carrier, climb to high altitude, and bomb the barge,
while observers marked the accuracy of the explosions.

In a short time all was ready, and the whine of the inertia
starters preceded the command: "Stand clear of propellers!"
Then "Start engines!" and the staccato bark of exhausts
swelled to muffled thunder as we warmed up our engines.
The planes ahead of me taxied out and took off.

Soon it was my turn. I headed up the deck, waited for the
"all clear" signal, and eased the throttle forward until it was
wide open. This was a heavy load, and I wanted plenty of
speed before I came to the end of the deck. My plane
gathered speed slowly, but I held it on until the end of the
deck was only a few yards ahead before I eased back on the
stick. The plane responded sluggishly, and seemed to stagger
off the deck into the air. The controls felt mushy, so I climbed
slowly, at a flat, conservative angle.

Finally I caught up with my section leader, and eased in
behind him in a careful join-up. One by one the others toiled
slowly up to join us, and the Skipper started the long climb
to dive-bombing altitude. Behind and below us the scout-
bombers started taking off with their 500-pounders.

As we continued the monotonous climb, I relaxed and began to be a little bit bored. This was just like any other flying.
Half an hour more, and we could get rid of these eggs and
head for home, I told myself. Let's see—what would I do next
weekend? Should I drive up to Los Angeles, or go down
to Tijuana with the gang? Or should I ————

Then without any preliminary call, a voice rang out over
the radio, an urgent call that jarred through my earphones
and shocked me back to attention: "Crash! Crash! Crash!"

Immediately there followed a confused babel of voices and
overlapping calls. For the moment, radio voice procedure was
forgotten: "Number Twelve has exploded and caught fire
. . ." " . . . at least three planes . . . " " . . . send the destroyers!" " . . . about two points off your starboard quarter . . ."
" . . . his 'chute did not open . . . " " . . . I think it was a
primer explosion . . . " " . . . Number Eleven and Number
Twelve . . . "

Glancing quickly around the horizon, I saw it. Several miles off to my left, a thick column of black smoke trailed down from our level to the ocean below. There was no motion to it whatever; it neither rose nor drifted. My eyes followed it down to its base, and there on the water burned the fierce bright flame of a gasoline fire. There was no wreckage visible—just that ominous pillar of black smoke with the fire at its base. Off to one side I could see the plane-guard destroyers rushing towards the spot at full speed, churning up a foaming white wake behind them. The carrier also circled in a wide turn and headed back.

What had happened? Who had crashed? What had caused it? A dozen questions flashed through my mind. Then one thought stood out like a bright white light that threw all the others into insignificance—one fragment of confused radio message rang in my ears: "I think it was a primer explosion . . ."

The idea loomed black and monstrous. *That* was it. The bombs must be defective. A bomb's primer, its sensitive detonating element, must have just exploded out there, blowing those planes out of the sky. And how many planes, the Lord only knew. And the rest of the bombs were probably defective too, and might let go any minute.

Apprehensively my eyes turned to the bomb that hung under my section leader's nearest wing. Suppose it should let go? Suppose a bomb on any plane in the squadron should let go? As close as we were, one bomb's explosion would probably jar off the next, and so on down the line, like a string of firecrackers. The whole squadron would be blown out of the sky.

Instinctively I edged away from my section leader with his

load of bombs. Then I noticed that the interval between the other planes had widened perceptibly; evidently the rest of the pilots were fearing the same thing. My throat grew dry and my hands clammy. How long was this suspense going to last?

Finally a welcome radio message came from the carrier: "Cease present exercise and return to base."

Our Skipper placed us in open formation and directed us to drop our bombs into the water. One after another, each plane peeled off from the formation and nosed over in a shallow dive. Pulling back the lever that armed my bombs, I placed the release lever on "salvo" and waited for the plane ahead of me to dive. After he had pulled clear, I shoved the stick forward, waited until my plane had gathered speed, jerked the bomb release toggle, and pulled up sharply, looking back over my shoulder to watch the bombs explode. Twin geysers of water spouted up as they hit, and the surrounding water was ripped and torn by flying fragments.

What a relief it was to be rid of that deadly burden! Quickly I joined the planes ahead of me, and soon the squadron was reunited—intact. Once more we flew our customary close formation, and confidence returned.

The flight back to the base was completed without incident, and back on the ground we anxiously asked for details of the accident. We learned that instead of being caused by detonating bombs, the disaster was the result of exploding fuel tanks, caused by an aerial collision between two planes during the join-up. Four men had gone down with the two planes, in water nearly a mile deep.

Under such circumstances, the bombing practice was discontinued—until daylight the next morning.

CHAPTER FOURTEEN

The East Coast

THE MONTHS SPED BY, AND AS THE END OF
the fiscal year approached we learned that the squadron was
to be transferred to the east coast. The Navy's newest aircraft carrier, the USS Enterprise, was about to be commissioned, and our squadron was to be attached to it as Fighting
Squadron Six. Several new officers were to join us, including
three new cadets, for about half of the officer personnel of
each squadron was now obtained from the aviation cadet
group.

Farewell parties in Coronado were the order of the day, as
we regretfully said goodbye to old friends, including half a
dozen of the senior officers who had been our section leaders
and wing mates for nearly a year. The Skipper left to take

command of a patrol squadron in Pearl Harbor, turning the
squadron command over to his executive officer, Lieutenant
Ward C. Gilbert. Others were transferred to stations from
Sitka to Coco Solo. Lieutenant Gouin went to Washington as
a naval aide on the President's staff. Lieutenant Symes had
been killed in a dive-bombing practice, and Lieutenant
Thorn was in the hospital with a collapsed lung, which kept
him there for nearly a year.

Several fatalities had occurred in other squadrons, but on
the whole the accident record was low for military flying. For
example, during the first four years there was not a single
fatality among the forty-odd members of my class who won
their wings. Whenever a fatality did occur, our minds merci-
fully refused to accept it as such. Friends were continually
being transferred to distant stations where we might never
see them again. We said goodbye, and they were gone out
of our lives. After a while, we thought of death the same way:
our friends had merely been transferred to more important
duty in the Final Squadron.

Again there was a month's leave between stations, and
once more I grew restless and anxious to get back to the
Navy long before it was time to report. Even a change of
scenery didn't help much, for when I ended up in New York
after three weeks at home, the city seemed to have lost its old
color and excitement. Finally the month was over, and I re-
joined the Squadron at Hampton Roads, Virginia, just outside
of Norfolk.

Our planes had been flown across the country by ferry
pilots from other squadrons while we were on leave, but in a
few days we had the squadron organized again and were
back in the air. Prior to the test runs of the Enterprise, we

made short cruises on her sister ship, the Yorktown, with refresher landings off the Virginia Capes. She was a grand ship,
boasting several new refinements in her gear and appointments, for unlike the Lexington and the Saratoga, which were
originally built as battle cruisers, the later carriers were all
designed from the first to carry airplanes.

The summer passed, and September rolled around. Football was in the air, and someone suggested a cross-country
flight to the next good game. The Skipper had a suggestion
that was even better. "Why don't you take in the National
Air Races at Cleveland?" he asked. "That's a real trip, and
you'd have a lot of fun."

We were delighted with the prospects, and my roommate
and I immediately put in a request for two fighters to make
the trip.

"Better refuel at Washington," suggested the Skipper, "in
case you have to back-track over the mountains. That stretch
of country is bad medicine. If things get tough, come on back
or sit down at the nearest airport. We don't want any
breakage."

The planes we were to take were the same Wasp-powered
Boeing F4B-4's, which were pretty well loaded down with
extra equipment, including tools, engine and cockpit covers,
a 55-gallon belly tank, 110 gallons of fuel, and all the clothes
we could cram into the so-called baggage compartment behind the narrow bucket seat.

All this extra equipment gave these planes a gliding range
in emergency landings which was not much greater than the
altitude. Consequently, we made our preparations very carefully. Beam coils were installed in our radio receivers. Although this meant sacrificing our inter-plane voice communi-

cation, it insured reception of weather broadcasts and gave us an additional check on our navigation.

Friday of that weekend dawned bright and clear, and we took off at eight o'clock. Salty, my roommate, led the way on the first leg to Washington while I tracked. Landing at the Anacostia Naval Air Station an hour later, we topped off our gasoline tanks and headed west towards Hagerstown, then to Buckstown, alternating the lead every half hour, checking our course on the clear, steady signals of the Buckstown radio beam.

As the prevailing winds were westerly, we were flying at the level of their lowest velocity, which was at 6,000 feet. However, an hour out of Washington, we observed scattered clouds at the 4,000-foot level, and it soon became evident that we would have to go below the clouds if we wanted to keep an eye on the ground. Since some of the ridges below us were topping the 2,000-foot level, it seemed advisable to get downstairs without delay.

Above the clouds the weather had been bright, clear, crisp, and blue; but as we descended into the condensation layer, the visibility decreased, the colors faded, and the sun's light dulled to a wan, sickly glow that reached us only intermittently through the gathering clouds above. Now and then a few scattered raindrops whisked across our windshields, and off to both sides we could see the misty columns of scattered rain squalls. The wooded hills below us had crept up to the 3,000-foot level, and the open spaces between the clouds above gradually filled in with mist until there was a solid overcast. I began to feel uneasy, in spite of the favorable weather forecast.

The ridges grew still higher, until an occasional hill had

its crest shrouded in mist, and once we followed a highway
through a deep valley with towering sides that reached up
into the overcast. The cars on the highway below were not
more than 500 feet beneath us as we skimmed along under
the ceiling.

At this point we could have turned back, except for the
fact that the highest mountains were now behind us, the
weather forecast ahead was favorable, and Pittsburgh was
only a few miles away. The rain squalls were increasing in
number and size, and although we barged right through most
of them, it was often necessary to detour around the larger
ones. A dim background of static in my earphones increased
in volume until it was hard to distinguish the signals of the
Pittsburgh radio beam ahead of us. But the city's proximity
was soon indicated by a pall of smoke, which blended with
the moisture in the air and further decreased the visibility.

As we approached the river area around Pittsburgh, the
hills sloped off rapidly until we had about 1,500 feet of altitude, and I began to breathe a bit easier. I was leading as we
crossed the river just north of the city, still on a compass
course for Cleveland, with plenty of gas left to get us there.
The static grew so bad that it drowned out all radio beam
signals, and I had to turn the volume down to save my ears.

Then I saw a momentary glow of lightning off to the right.
A few miles farther, and the flashes were plainly visible. We
seemed to be south of the disturbance, so I held my course.
West of the city the smoke cleared, the ceiling lifted to about
2,000 feet, and the visibility increased until we could see five
or six miles ahead.

The lightning flashes on our right were now bright and
vivid, playing through a great cloud-bank that seemed to run

from west to east. A few minutes later we saw lightning directly ahead, and as we progressed we found ourselves confronted by a solid wall of threatening black clouds, advancing before a thick curtain of rain.

Hoping that the storm was a local one, I turned left and headed south along the wall of clouds for a few miles, trying to skirt the edge. Conditions there were even worse. The cloud front was advancing rapidly. There seemed to be no end to it, and the lightning was almost continuous.

Looking back over my shoulder, I saw that Salty was flying close above me, with a worried expression on his face visible even through his goggles. He pointed to the storm and shook his head. I nodded, pointing back towards Pittsburgh. He nodded enthusiastically, patting his windshield to indicate increased speed. I shoved my throttle forward to maximum allowable manifold pressure, kicked hard left rudder, and high-tailed it back east towards Pittsburgh.

Glancing at the strip-map on my navigation board, I picked out the nearest airport and set my course for it, racing ahead of the storm. The visibility decreased as we reached the smoky area, so I switched on my running lights and followed the course of the river which runs through the center of the city. We could always sit down on the water if the storm closed in, and our flotation gear would save the planes. It was better than trying to climb up through the stuff, finally having to jump, and letting a two-ton plane go plunging down into a highly populated area.

The river led us directly to the business section of the city, where it forked around the skyscraper district. Taking the south fork, I followed it until we were due north of the airport, according to the map. The rain was just behind us, white and solid. There was no time for any mistakes in dead reckoning.

According to my rapid calculations, if we headed south for five minutes, we should be about over the airport. If we missed, we would be out of luck, for the visibility was not more than half a mile.

Taking a deep breath, I swung the ship around to the right until the compass was on south, meanwhile keeping one eye on the clock. Allowing for a westerly wind, the airport should appear out of the gloom on my right. As the minutes crawled by, I scanned the ground anxiously, but no airport appeared. I began to doubt the accuracy of my navigation, the map, the compass, the airspeed meter—everything.

I glanced back at Salty. He was dipping his wings violently, and pointing frantically to the left. There below us was the biggest asphalt landing mat I had ever seen, with a huge administration building at the edge, and off at one corner some hangars with the familiar black-and-yellow markings of the Army's Air Corps. The landing mat was as big as all outdoors; it looked as if half the county was paved, and the Army hangars were like a big sign that said "Welcome!"

We circled for a landing on this ideal airport. The runways, which allowed for every wind direction, were as wide as the length of the average auxiliary field, and so long that they seemed to stretch almost to the horizon. This effect was accentuated by the location of the airport on top of a ridge higher than any of the surrounding area, giving an unobstructed approach to any of the runways. It was like landing on the deck of a carrier in the open sea, with none of the high tension wires, buildings, or tanks that usually surround most airports to make pilots gray-haired. The Army hangars were actually below the surface of the field, down at the base of the hill. A more ideal arrangement would be hard to imagine.

We set our ships down on the smooth asphalt and taxied up in front of the Army operations office. Here we were met by the commanding officer, Major Smith, who led the way in his car while we taxied behind him down a long ramp at the edge of the field into roomy hangars below, just before the rain hit. There was plenty of wind in the storm that followed.

"Which way are you headed?" asked the Major.

"West, to Cleveland," we replied.

"Then you'd better come on up and take it easy. It's pretty bad west of here, and I don't think we'll be able to clear you today."

Our hopes sank. No Cleveland, no Air Races. Here we were, stuck out in the sticks, with the nearest hotel probably fifteen miles away in Pittsburgh. The next weather reports only confirmed the Major's diagnosis. Weather conditions, if anything, were getting worse. Our faces were a yard long.

"Cheer up!" laughed the Major. "The Air Races will last three more days, and you've got plenty of company. There were four other service ships in here ahead of you, and they're all grounded. Hop into our station wagon, and we'll drive you over to the airport restaurant for a bite to eat, then take you over to the Flyer's Club."

That night the Flyer's Club was nearly filled with weather-bound pilots, for the ceiling came right down to the ground. It would have been hard to assemble a more complete assortment of pilots on such short notice. The guest register listed Army, Coast Guard, Navy, National Guard, Marine Corps, airline, and private pilots. Two airline hostesses shared the women's section with a girl pilot from Washington who came in with a tri-motored Stinson. There were all types of planes grounded at the airport, from the giant transports down to our little single-seaters.

A pall of gloom descended on the lively group at the club when we learned that an Army observation plane had crashed on the ridge just east of Pittsburgh while trying to get through the bad weather, killing pilot and passenger.

Rain and fog made a dismal night, but we all gathered together in the comfortable living-room, brought in the tall glasses, broke out the Gloom Chaser, and swapped stories. Each group had something to contribute in the way of flying experience that was interesting to the others, and we talked far into the night.

The next morning after a refreshing sleep, we went over to the airport to check the weather reports. Here we found the airline weather bureau's facilities as open to military and civilian pilots as it was to company employees.

Complete and accurate weather data, supplementing that given us by the Army's aerological department, enabled us to make Cleveland that afternoon.

The National Air Race Committee outdid anything we had ever seen in the way of hospitality. They provided mechanics for our planes, gave us box seats for the races, put us up at a good hotel in Cleveland, and entertained us like visiting potentates the whole weekend. They introduced us to the president of a women's pilot organization which was holding a convention in Cleveland, and we attended their banquet and the military ball which followed. Salty became quite enthusiastic about one of the "lady pilots" as he called them, until I began to wonder if I was going to have to fly home alone. It was a glorious weekend.

When it was time to leave, our thoughts turned again to Pittsburgh, and we scheduled that city as our first stop. "Maybe the weather will be bad," said Salty hopefully, "and maybe some of the lady pilots will be there."

It was, and they were. And by some strange, inexplicable coincidence, most of the pilots we had met there before also decided to stop over at Pittsburgh. It was like Old Home Week. Major Smith, who met us as usual with the Army's grand hospitality, did not appear to be surprised at our return. "We were expecting you!" he said with a grin.

The Major finally got rid of us by clearing us on the radio beams over a lot of thick soup to Harrisburg, where we spiraled down through a hole and flew contact to Washington. From there a 700-foot ceiling was ample to get us over the intervening flat country to Norfolk. The Skipper, who had been reading the weather reports apprehensively, was relieved when we got back without any "breakage," leaving the squadron intact for the gunnery season.

A few days later, I was to be responsible for the first "breakage" that had been chalked up against me in more than two years of flying for the Navy.

CHAPTER FIFTEEN

High Speed Approach

THE FOLLOWING MONDAY WE STARTED GUN-nery practice, using the open Atlantic off Virginia Beach for our firing range. After our record rehearsal with fixed guns we shifted the squadron's operating area to Whitehurst Farm, near the air station, with a bombing target laid out nearby.

The first day's practice was uneventful. We started our dives from a comparatively low altitude below five thousand feet, which was a lucky thing for me a little later. The next day was my birthday, and when we took off to fly out and load our bomb-racks at Whitehurst Farm, the bright blue October morning was exhilarating, and I felt as cocky as a twelve-year-old boy just entering his teens.

When we reached the field I peeled off from the formation, glanced down casually to see which way the others were landing, and started my approach. The bomb-loading crew was at the far end of the field, so instead of setting my plane down short and taxying the rest of the way as the others had done, I picked out a spot near the last third of the field and went through the motions of landing.

But in some perverse manner, the tail of the little ship refused to come down. This was a bit disconcerting, so I kicked hard rudder and fishtailed to lose some of my excess flying speed before the wheels touched. When they did, the tail was still in the air and I was only a few hundred feet from the edge of the field. Under ordinary circumstances, this would have been plenty of room, but just to play safe, I started to give her the gun and go around the field again for another try. And then I remembered the power line, dead ahead of me.

From that moment I knew I had to go through with it, bad landing or no. Applying the brakes as hard as I dared, I went bumping across the rapidly diminishing remainder of the field, still tail-high. Ahead of me was an asphalt road with a row of houses on the far side. The road was open, and my hopes rose as I saw that there were no drainage ditches. I might be able to turn down the road, if I could slow down enough before I reached it. I eased on the brakes until the wheels were locked, but the tires slid right along over the dew-covered grass.

At the road I was confronted with a dilemma that required a quick decision: I could either kick hard rudder and ground-loop the plane, which would probably dish in a wing and wash out the landing gear, or I could go straight between a power-line pole and one of the houses, which would give me a few extra yards in a flower garden to stop rolling.

Every pilot instinctively hates ground loops, and I am no exception: I went straight ahead. At the edge of the road I felt the brakes take hold, and managed to turn just the amount necessary to miss the front porch of the house without dragging a wing. I thought I had her stopped, but the right wheel dug into a shallow depression and the tail rose slowly, majestically, until the prop bit into the sandy loam and the plane came to rest on the two front wheels and the tip of the propeller.

There is no feeling on earth that can compare with the embarrassment and shame that floods over you like a hot wave when you nose up an airplane. The thing sits there with its tail ignominiously high in the air, a signal for everyone in the vicinity to gather around and jeer you on your throne of disgrace. And the rest of the squadron didn't neglect the opportunity. They hurried over as fast as they could cut their switches.

"Nice three-point landing!" one observed casually.

"What's the idea, couldn't you wait to pick those flowers?" asked another.

"Maybe you'll land short and taxi after this, like the rest of us common folks!" said a third.

The Skipper eyed the plane critically. "I'm very sorry you had to undergo this experience, Bob," he told me quietly. "We'll send you another prop on the squadron truck."

That was all. If he'd only bawled me out, I wouldn't have minded. We changed the propeller, which had a bent tip, and I flew the ship back to the base, vowing that I would use the entire field forever after. The Trouble Board gave me fifty per cent wet grass, but that couldn't dull my own feeling that it was one hundred per cent dumb pilot.

The gunnery officer was sympathetic. "Cheer up," he said. "You flew it home, didn't you?"

"Yes, but I hate to admit that you've got such a sap for an assistant," I answered. "That just cuts me out of a whole day's bombing practice until they can check the engine."

"We've got a week of practice left," he told me. "One of us has to observe from the ground today anyway, so it will work out all right. You just drive on out to the bombing target and forget about that bent prop."

So off I went, to join the ground crew at the observing station, where I soon forgot about everything but keeping a whole hide.

Although I had dropped bombs many times, this was the first time I had ever been in the path of a dive bomber when it was really in action. Of course the bombs were only miniatures about a foot long, with a blank charge of powder to mark the point of impact with a puff of white smoke, but the planes were starting their dives nearly a mile above the target and the bombs were travelling so fast by the time they struck that we had to dig down through four feet of solid earth to find one. To get some idea of the force of their impact, remember that a couple of sandbags will stop a bullet from an army rifle.

We had a "bombproof" shelter made of heavy timbers piled high with sandbags, where we could mark the drops with comparative safety, but the ordnancemen were standing casually out in the open, retiring to the shelter only when it was obvious that the diving planes were headed in their general direction. The first time a plane dived, I was standing about ten feet from the shelter talking to another pilot who was observing the practice. I saw only the first part of the dive. For some mysterious reason, I suddenly found myself crouching beneath the shelter, and I bumped heads with my friend on the way in. Neither of us remembered starting for the shelter. The bomb struck over a hundred yards away, and the ordnancemen gave us the merry ha-ha.

The next plane started its dive, and I resolved firmly not to move unless I was directly in the line of the dive. My friend did likewise. Nevertheless, we found ourselves back in the shelter several seconds before the bomb struck, even though it hit farther away than the first one. The plane swept by with a sinister, snarling roar that made the shelter vibrate even though the pilot was more than a thousand feet overhead.

"Whew!" exclaimed the other pilot. "No wonder they can't make ground troops stand up and shoot at a plane in a dive-bombing or strafing attack! I would have sworn that baby was headed right for us!"

"Me too," I agreed, reflecting that in war time the fragments of even such distant drops might have clipped us.

After watching carefully for an hour or so, we finally were able to tell approximately when the bombs would not strike near us, but if there was any doubt in our minds, we scrambled into the shelter with no regard for traffic rules.

Many of the pilots, considering that the bombs were released when the target was over a quarter of a mile below, achieved considerable accuracy. If they had ever come down out of the sun-lane at any vulnerable target, even though it was protected by gunfire, most of them would have made direct hits.

To my mind, there is no other form of flying that will compare with dive bombing at a make-believe "enemy" target. The competition between squadrons is keen, and the individual pilot with the lowest score who brings down his squadron's rating usually has to buy the beer. The average pilot is uncomfortable only in prolonged dives from extremely high altitudes; under ten thousand feet the sensation is exhilarating, even in a terminal velocity dive. No other sport offers such a feeling of projection, for the very attitude of your plane, which becomes only an extension of yourself, is the factor which determines your accuracy.

A lot of bilge has been written about the tremendous bodily stresses that pilots undergo in this work, but the fact is that the human body can be subjected to stresses that will wrench the wings off the sturdiest airplane; consequently pilots are careful not to impose even enough strain on the plane during the pull-out to cause themselves to "black out." The feeling is more like sliding down an oiled groove with a wide sweeping curve at the bottom. Of course the engine roars and the wires sing, but the pilot is usually so intent on lining up his sights that he pays no attention to it. The propeller noise, which is responsible for most of the atrocious racket heard by the observers, is flung outward away from the plane and is almost inaudible to the pilot.

The next day the gunnery officer notified me that my engine was undamaged when I nosed it over the day before and that the plane was all set for bombing. "Let's see you go out there and get some hits," he told me.

So out I went, this time being careful to use all of the field for my landings. Although the auxiliary field we were using to load the bombs was not a large one, there was a strong wind blowing which made it easy to land short that day.

I took on a load of bombs and climbed up with the others to the 5000-foot level. The planes which we were flying, F4B-4's, had a terminal velocity lower than the cruising speed of some modern planes in level flight. I was soon to have reason to be thankful for this.

The wind grew stronger with the altitude, which made our bombs fall short on the up-wind approaches, wide on the cross-wind dives, and over the mark on down-wind drops. I had only two bombs left when the gunnery officer's voice came over the radio: "Fighting Six planes from Six Fox Four: cease bombing after the next round until high winds subside."

The next approach was down-wind. Pushing over a bit late, I picked up the target in the center of my telescope sight only when I was in a very steep dive. Instinct told me not to release the bomb, as the wind had carried me on past the target before I was halfway down. Soon I was past the vertical, hanging by my safety belt, with the sights still pointed back towards the target. But this was my last round, and I wanted to see how far past the target the bomb would fall.

I pulled the bomb-release toggle. Instantly there was a tremendous grinding roar, followed by a terrific vibration of the entire plane. The little ship seemed to slow down in the dive. I chopped the throttle and eased up in the steepest pull-out I could make without going black, fighting to conserve all the altitude I had. The whole plane was shaking so hard that the wheels were fluttering through an arc wide enough for me to see them above the lower wing, several inches above their normal position. There was no doubt in my mind what had happened: the bomb had taken off part of the propeller, and the resulting vibration was shaking the plane to pieces.

Three long cracks appeared in the shatterproof glass of the windshield in front of my eyes. As the plane lost speed, I saw that I had managed to level out at nearly two thousand feet. That gave me time to think. Holding the stick back, I found that the plane tended to fall off in a spin with the throttle closed. I eased the throttle forward tentatively, and immediately chopped it back when the vibration resumed. With the throttle opened just a few notches, I found that I could maintain flying speed if I kept the plane in a very steep glide.

All this took me down to about 1500 feet, where I was confronted with the time-worn dilemma: should I try to save the ship or should I bail out and walk home? I could still make the field *if* I didn't overshoot or *if* the engine didn't fall off its mountings from the shaking it had taken. If I made the field, I would be safe, *if* the flopping landing gear didn't collapse when the wheels touched the ground. If it did—well, the slowest glide I could hold was about eighty knots, which would be uncomfortably fast for a cartwheel crash. I unbuckled my safety belt, getting ready to jump.

And if I jumped . . . Glancing over the side, I saw a dozen planes parked on the field below. There was a cluster of houses around a grocery store at the corner of the field. The pilotless plane might wreck two or three others or wipe out a whole family. I snapped my safety belt back in place and headed for the field. The altimeter showed 900 feet. Pushing my microphone button, I called into the radio transmitter: "Fighting Six planes from Six Fox Nine: stay clear of the field. Am making emergency landing!"

Here was the forced landing I'd been training for all these years. Would I make it? The thought never crossed my mind; I was too busy figuring wind velocity, angle of glide, distance to the field, and all of the dozen variables which would bring me down where I wanted to go. The strong wind was in my favor, for it would slow me down and shorten the roll after I touched. The steep angle of glide was a big help, for I could now clear the power line without side-slipping, which might spin me in with that freakish gliding speed. It finally resolved simply into hugging the edge of the field until I was just high enough to clear the wires and then diving straight in.

Leveling off as close to the ground as I could, I cut the switch, eased the stick back, and braced myself with one hand to keep my face out of the instrument panel. To my surprise and relief, the landing gear held, and a normal landing followed. I noted with satisfaction that I still had a few hundred feet of field left. Then I climbed out of the cockpit to take a look at the plane. Half of one propeller blade had been sheared off by the steel bomb, which had dented the trailing edge of the other blade. The bent edges may have been responsible for the curious gliding effects I had noticed.

Standing on tip-toe, I reached up to touch the ragged edge of the prop. When I stepped back, I found that I could not get my heels back on the ground, and my knees began to shake violently. The more I tried to control them, the harder they shook. This was the first reaction to the strain that I noticed, and it soon passed.

Two other planes landed and taxied up.

"Nice going," drawled the first pilot. "What are you trying for, a plane a day?"

"If you destroy any more American planes," said the other, "we're going to give you an Iron Cross and make you a German Ace!"

Again we changed the prop and checked up the engine, which miraculously was unharmed. I flew it back to the base and went shamefacedly in to report to the Skipper, who puffed quietly away at his cigar while I told him what had happened. I fully expected to be grounded for a month. "Let me see," he said, looking out through the window, "didn't you get a new prop only yesterday?"

"Yes, sir," I admitted.

"And you've got a new one today?"

"That's right, sir."

"Well, that makes three. You've had your quota for this week. Get along now, and let's see you be a little more careful with this one!"

CHAPTER SIXTEEN

New Thunderbirds

AT NORFOLK THE BACHELOR OFFICERS' QUAR-
ters were right at the edge of the main landing field, so that
planes taking off or landing often passed by only a few yards
overhead. We grew so accustomed to this noise that we paid
no attention to it, and could even sleep soundly while night
flying was in progress. But one day during lunch we heard
a new sound, a high-pitched, snarling roar that filled the sky
and shook the mess hall. Everyone stopped eating and looked
up; this was no ordinary airplane.

Several of us rushed to the door and looked out to see a
blunt-nosed, heavy fighter with the biggest engine we had
ever seen in a single-seater, circling the field for an approach.
"It's an F3F-*Two*!" cried one. "Our new planes are coming!"

"Golly, look at that engine!" exclaimed another. "A thousand horses, and all for *one man*!"

And so it was. This was the first of our new Grumman
fighters, powered by the same G-Series Wright Cyclone
engines that the biggest airliners used—the latest and fastest
shipboard fighters in the Navy. Lunch was forgotten. We all
rushed over to inspect the new arrival as the pilot taxied in,

marvelling at the size of the plane and the roominess of the cockpit. It had everything in the way of the most advanced equipment, including a constant-speed three-blade propeller, adjustable trim tabs for all flight controls, retractable landing gear, and a complete set of the latest aids for instrument flying.

We lost no time in checking out in these new beauties, and it was a treat to fly them. A take-off in one was the biggest thrill I had experienced since my last catapult shot. There was the same feeling of being launched into space by a steady, irresistible force. The controls were even more sensitive than in the lighter F4B-4's. If we held these planes near the ground on the take-off until they reached the edge of the field and then hauled back on the stick, they would zoom almost straight up for over a thousand feet—a vertical climb at nearly a mile a minute.

But they were bigger and heavier than any single-seater we had flown, and we treated them with a lot of respect. A couple of the newer pilots, junior grade lieutenants fresh out of Pensacola, got into trouble at the start. One switched his gasoline selector valve to the wrong tank as he circled the field, and the engine cut out. When the pilot saw he could not make the field, he set the plane down in rough water just off shore. The flotation compartments were ruptured and the plane started to sink. The pilot inflated his pneumatic life raft, but the wind carried it away from him and he was picked up by a small boat just as he started to sink.

The other pilot brought his plane in over the wires at Whitehurst Farm in a power stall and chopped his throttle as he had been accustomed to doing in the lighter training planes. The nose of the plane dropped from the weight of the heavy engine and the plane dove into the ground, flopping over on its back and pinning the pilot in the cockpit with gasoline dripping all over him. The pilot was uninjured, but the next day he submitted a request for sea duty and turned in his wings.

A few days later we lost another plane and with it one of the newly reported cadets. Three of us had gone out on familiarization flights. We had been instructed to practice acrobatics and to try a few dives, but to avoid spins. An hour later when I returned, two other pilots met me at the line with astonished expressions. "We heard you had just been killed in a crash at Virginia Beach!" they told me.

"Who was it?" I asked.

"We don't know. They said it was you, but it must have been Boyd or Peabody."

A short time later we saw Peabody's plane approaching, and knew then that we had lost Charley Boyd, one of the most popular pilots in the squadron. The reason for the crash was never determined, but from the swath the plane had cut through the trees, it appeared that the pilot had pulled out too low after a dive.

These incidents only increased our respect for the equipment we were using, and we doubled our precautions. As a result, there were no more crashes in our squadron during the rest of the year I spent at Norfolk.

The improved performance we were able to get out of the Grummans developed new tactics. Once or twice a week the Skipper would lead us out in squadron formation for an hour of maneuvers that included everything in the book and a few new tricks we hadn't seen before.

One morning as we walked into the squadron office there

was the usual cluster of pilots around the mimeograph machine waiting for copies of the daily flight schedule.

"What's on the program today?" asked one, peering over the yeoman's shoulder.

"Long-range practice in the morning, both guns," was the answer, "and squadron tactics in the afternoon."

"Squadron tactics, hey?" repeated the pilot. "I nearly got my tail feathers clipped when I doped off for a second in the last rat race."

"Yeah, there's never a dull moment," said another, "especially since we got the new ships."

He was right. When you get eighteen pilots in single-seaters, each with a 1000-horsepower engine that is sufficient to keep an eighteen-passenger transport in the air, flying tight formation at three miles a minute, and diving in mass maneuvers at twice that speed, there never *is* a dull moment.

The regular air station field at Norfolk was being repaired, and our squadron was based temporarily at the small auxiliary field at the west end of the Naval Operating Base. The West Field was in fairly good shape for a grass covered sand base, but it was none too large, with buildings on two sides and three big storage tanks in one corner filled with 87 octane aviation gasoline—liquid dynamite that gave us cold shivers every time we saw a formation take off or land in that quadrant of the compass.

That afternoon there was hardly a breath of air stirring, but fortunately it was from the open portion of the field, which lies right at the water's edge, not far from the scene of the historic encounter between the Merrimac and the Monitor. Taxying out to leeward as far as possible so as to use the entire field, we took off by sections, three planes at a time.

I was in the third section, in plane Number Nine. Lining up on the right of my section leader, who flew Number Seven, I glanced over my instruments as I checked them against the printed list in the cockpit, locking my tail-wheel, setting my stabilizer at the take-off angle, adjusting my propeller-pitch control for maximum r.p.m., and assuring myself that the half-dozen other items were properly arranged.

This done, I raised my left hand as a signal to the section leader that I was ready to go. He raised his left hand and glanced at the other wing man, who also had his left hand raised. As the section leader lowered his hand, I did the same, placing it on the throttle, which I gradually eased forward. The plane started rolling, gathering speed so fast that by the time I had my throttle barely open, the tail was in the air. Out of the corner of my eye I saw Number Seven's wheels leave the ground, and eased back on my stick just a trifle. The bouncing sensation turned to one of steady, smooth acceleration, and the three planes lifted as one.

As the edge of the field swept by below, I rolled up my retractable landing gear, set my stabilizer and rudder trim controls until the ship was flying hands off, and relaxed. The slightest touch on the stick now put the ship anywhere I wanted it, and a similar touch of the throttle increased or decreased the interval between me and the section leader, who swept in a wide climbing turn towards his rendezvous with the first two sections aloft. Gradually he eased up into position, with so imperceptible a movement of the controls that all I felt was a slight pressure of my right foot against the rudder pedal. The section moved magically into position above and to the right of the other two sections—a right echelon of V's. A short time later I glanced up to see the second division of nine planes above us in the same formation.

The Skipper, at the head of the procession, gave the signal for a V of V's, and again our section slid effortlessly across and eased down into place. A moment later, the wing man passed along the Skipper's signal for a division V, and I lifted my plane literally with my fingertips and eased it up over Number Seven until I was on the extreme end of a giant V. Glancing down below us to the waters of Chesapeake Bay, I saw the squadron's shadow skimming across the surface, two giant chevrons that hurtled along like twin arrowheads in outline.

Next came a signal that required a little more delicate execution—the division line. I glanced at the man in the plane directly across from me on the opposite end of the V. We both had to arrive on a line with the Skipper's plane at exactly the same instant, if the maneuver was to be executed properly, so that the V gradually opened out to a straight line of planes with their wings only a few feet apart. The other pilots slowly pulled up into line, and as I reached position I could look straight across and see the opposite wing man lining up with the others—nine planes cruising along at three miles a minute, with their wing tips so close together that a man almost could step from one to the other, if it were not for the wind blast. The second division was in a similar line just above.

The Skipper glanced from side to side until he was satisfied that all planes were in position, and then cruised along with the line of planes undulating slightly in the varying air currents over the bay. I felt myself tensing up with the strain of making the delicate control adjustments necessary to main-

tain my position on the end of the line, and forced myself
to relax. Then the Skipper eased ahead with his throttle, and
the inside men did the same, stretching the line back to its
original V shape. This gave me a chance to lift my goggles
for a moment to let the refreshing air a mile above the earth
cool my face.

At the next signal, I crossed back over my wing man, and
the division was again in a V of V's. A slight pressure of
my right foot on the rudder pedal was necessary to keep in
position 45 degrees on my section leader's starboard quarter,
which told me that he was again on the move, and a moment
later I saw the other two sections slide by below us, leaving
the squadron in a right echelon of V's.

Then the Skipper gave the attack signal, and I knew we
were in for a section dive. Adjusting my stabilizer and rudder
control tabs, I tightened my safety belt and got set for it.
The first two sections dropped out of sight. My section leader
gradually pushed the blunt nose of his ship over, over and
still over, until we seemed to be past the vertical. I stood
on my rudder pedals to brace myself as we picked up speed
in a breath-taking dive. Gravity went into reverse, and I was
pressed upward against my safety belt, while particles of
dust and sand floated up around me from the bottom of the
cockpit.

Meanwhile I was centering all my effort trying to keep
in position. I started to over-run my section leader, and eased
back on the throttle, wondering how it could have any effect
during the screaming, roaring rush of the dive. A super-hur-
ricane pressed with such deadly weight upon my plane's
wings that the stick forces needed for control were increased
ten-fold. As the landscape leaped to meet us it expanded,

swelled, and spread out until I wanted to haul back on the stick and pull out before we were smashed deep into the earth itself.

Just as it seemed that no power could save us, there was a gradual tilt of the panorama below. Still flying on my section leader, I felt my weight gradually return to normal, until it was pressing back where it belonged on my parachute pack. There was a click in my ears as they adjusted themselves to the change in altitude. Then the horizon came into view, the snarl in the wires faded away, and we zoomed half a mile upward on the momentum of that wild dive. My heart beat faster and a strange exhilaration gripped me as I drew in a deep, satisfying breath. We had made it.

A minute later the squadron had again effected a rendezvous in a right echelon of V's. The Skipper signaled for a squadron echelon of echelons, and the left wing men crossed over to form a long stairway—eighteen planes so close together that their wings and tails overlapped. A slight gust of wind caught the leader, and there was a momentary accordion movement as each successive plane flew through it. The squadron steadied down for a moment, then as I glanced down along the row of heads I saw the Skipper suddenly peel off from the formation and nose over in a vertical dive. The others followed so fast that there were only a few yards between planes in the dive, and I knew that we were in for one of the most exciting thrills that aviation has to offer—a game of follow-the-leader with an entire squadron of planes.

As I followed the planes ahead, they strung out in a long dive that curved at the bottom where the Skipper zoomed up until his plane was ready to stall, then straightened out

in a chandelle that left the procession of planes turning behind him at exactly the same place his ship had turned. From
here the Skipper nosed down to pick up speed and then
banked up into a long wing-over, so that on the zoom I
passed close to the planes in the second division on their way
down. Soon there were three rows of diving and climbing
planes passing each other in a progressive wing-over that
ended only when the Skipper straightened out in a long,
sweeping dive that curved up and over. As I went over the
top I glanced down and saw that the whole squadron was in
a loop—a vertical circle a quarter of a mile in diameter.

At the bottom of his loop the Skipper straightened out in
another dive a little faster than the first, then zoomed up
and over on his back in the beginning of another loop. But
this time he slowly half-rolled his plane out in a perfect Immelman turn, right behind the tail end of the procession, so
that when I looked down as I hung by my safety-belt I saw
the last plane start to zoom from the bottom of its dive.

Glancing at my altimeter, I noted with surprise that I had
gained several thousand feet in these maneuvers, thanks to
the thousand horses pounding away in the Cyclone. From
10,000 feet, the Skipper banked around in a wide circle,
closing up until he was directly behind plane Number Eighteen. I was banked up on my side in a vertical turn, fighting
vicious slip streams that struck my plane and spun it half
around before I could kick hard rudder and haul back on
the stick with both hands as I tried to stay in position. As
the circle wound up I could actually hear the propellers of
the other planes—a sound rarely heard in the air. The slip
streams were soon so violent that I saw one plane after another spin out of the circle and climb back up into position.

Suddenly my plane was knocked over on its back, in spite of all my efforts to control it, and I blasted on full gun until I could regain my place in this mad tail-chase.

Then the Skipper dipped his nose and started down in a wide, easy spiral with each plane following until I could look down into the vortex of a winding maelstrom of whirling propellers and spiralling ships. The centrifugal force of this continued spiral wedged me down into my seat and made my arms and legs as heavy as in a nightmare, so that it required a determined effort to lift my hand to the throttle, until the Skipper leveled out and waved his flippers as a signal that the maneuvers were over.

As each section entered the lane of home-bound traffic at the thousand-foot level, the wing men dropped back and crossed over to a right echelon. This field was too small for a section landing, especially with that day's almost no-wind condition. As I lowered my landing gear and ran through the landing check-off list, I glanced at the wind-tee from force of habit. This time the breeze had decided to be perverse and stay right where it was when we took off, probably because that was the worst possible approach for a landing at West Field—right over the high-test gasoline storage tanks.

When the section broke up I took plenty of interval for an unobstructed approach, as low over the tanks as I dared. Holding the nose of the ship up, I came ahead in a power stall. If my engine quit just now, over those tanks . . . but I dismissed the thought. Now I was safely past the last obstruction. And as I taxied up to the line where my mechanic waved me the "All clear!" sign, I was still tingling with the sensations of the last hour, for anything else I had ever done before in my life was tame by comparison.

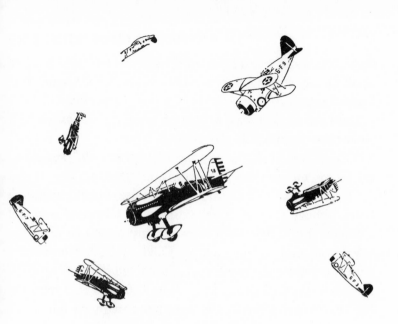

CHAPTER SEVENTEEN

Feud with the Army

We don't have to march like the infantry
Ride like the cavalry, shoot like the artillery
And we can lick your whole damn Army
For we are the old Nay-vee!
     —Air: The Old Gray Mare

JUST ACROSS HAMPTON ROADS A FEW MILES
north of Newport News was Langley Field, the great eastern
base of the Army Air Corps. Except for an occasional visit to
their experimental laboratories, where the N. A. C. A. (National Advisory Committee for Aeronautics) conducted wind-
tunnel tests on all service airplanes, we saw very little of the
Army's aviators.

One morning however, we noticed a couple of Army pursuit planes cruising around over the Naval Air Station, and a

short time later one of our pilots strode into the squadron ready-room, cussing a blue streak. "Those blankety-blank Army buzzards!" he growled. "A couple of them in P-6's jumped me while I was out testing our old O2U, and nearly forced me down in Chesapeake Bay!

"Maybe we ought to pay them a return call," suggested Ed Burke, one of the first cadets in the squadron.

"That's a good idea," said "Red" Hulse, another cadet. "I know a shavetail over there. Suppose we telephone him that if they want to play, we'll meet 'em any place they like."

Red put in a call to Langley Field, and returned shortly with the news that the Army had accepted the challenge. "It was my old pal, all right," he grinned. "He says he'll meet any one of us at noon over the James River Bridge. He'll be at six thousand feet in a P-6."

"He's my meat!" said Burke. "I thought of it first!"

"Fine!" agreed Red. "But this lad has a crude sense of humor, and he's probably cooking up a surprise party. A couple of us will tag along behind you, just in case there's any funny business. We'll stay up above you out of sight, and won't come down unless they start something."

All of us wanted to see the fun, and just to make certain that we would not be caught napping, we finally decided to have an extra section of planes off to one side in case the first three were outnumbered. So three of us took off ahead of the others and climbed to twelve thousand feet, where we cruised around in a wide circle over the appointed rendezvous, watching to see what would happen. A short time later we saw Hulse and Babson circling a few thousand feet below us, and then Burke's plane came into view, barely visible against the background of water below.

As we watched, another plane came out from the north to meet Burke, and a routine dogfight ensued. But a few minutes later we saw two other planes climbing to join the fracas, and knew that they must be Army reinforcements. Below us, the two planes from our own squadron nosed over and started down, engaging the attacking army planes before they could climb to the level of the original duel. Then Tom Bradbury, who was flying ahead of me, pointed off below us and to one side, and I saw another section of the Army's early vintage Curtiss Hawks approaching at the eight thousand foot level. The leader rocked his wings, and the three planes started down to get in on the fun.

Nosing over in a steep dive, we lost no time going down, and soon we were in the midst of the wildest, craziest, dizziest melee I had ever been mixed up in. Only twelve planes were involved, but the air seemed to be full of them, all paired off in individual dogfights, diving and zooming, milling around in overlapping circles, every man hell-bent on riding his opponent's tail and forcing him down. How we ever avoided hitting each other is a mystery.

Our planes were newer and faster than the comparatively obsolete Hawks, but the latter had a shorter turning radius which gave them a disconcerting advantage as the fight gradually worked down to a lower altitude. Only when the Army pilots made the mistake of trying to outdive us was there a decisive advantage in our favor. The Army's Hawks had conventional landing gear, while the wheels on our Grummans were retractable. Whenever a Hawk entered a dive, one of our planes was on his tail like a streamlined brick, and there was no getting away. I followed my man down almost to the water, where he leveled off and slowed down until I could fly up alongside. He grinned and clasped his hands above his head, and the fight was over. I waved in answer and zoomed up to watch the rest of the fight.

One after another, the individual dogfights were fought to some sort of a conclusion. Burke followed his man down and chased him right across Langley Field, until the Army pilot covered his face with his arm to indicate engine trouble, and sideslipped into the field for a dead-stick landing.

A short time later we met in a rendezvous and started for home, but on the way back a couple of us took time out to "dust off" an Army A-17 attack plane that was cruising peace-fully towards Langley Field. When we returned to the squad-ron there was a telephone call for Red, who found his Army friend on the wire. It appeared that we had carried our fun a bit too far: two of the Army planes had limped home with engine trouble, and the pilot of the attack plane had been a major who was practicing instrument flying under the hood when we dived on him. "The major claims you nearly spun him in," said the Army pilot. "He's pretty mad about it. What shall I tell him?"

"Tell him we thought they were Marines," said Red, "and tell him the pilot who did it was a lieutenant commander."

This explanation apparently mollified the major, but the feud was on. The next day three Army attack planes caught one of our pilots at a low altitude and forced him down in a small emergency field at Virginia Beach. We retaliated by diving on one of their four-engined flying fortresses until the pilots waved us away. For a few days any of us who ventured out alone could count on having a couple of Army planes circling high above the Air Station waiting to dive on his tail.

The activity ceased as suddenly as it had begun. Burke and

Dzendolet cruised around Langley Field one morning making as much noise as they could with their propellers in low pitch, daring the Army pilots to come out and fight. Ordinarily this challenge would have had plenty of response in a few minutes, but this time no Army pursuit ships taxied out to take off. On their return we had a telephone call from Red's friend at Langley Field. "Call off your dogs, will you?" he asked with a laugh. "Our staff got wind of what has been going on and read the riot act to us. No more dogfights, or we'll all be grounded."

And so we had to call it quits. We made arrangements to have our Army friends over for a beer party, but a cross-country tour took us away for several days, and on our return we left for another cruise on the Yorktown, so that I never had the pleasure of meeting our comrades in arms.

Some time later the Skipper asked for volunteers to ferry several of our old F4B-4's back to Pensacola. Since winter had set in, this seemed like a good chance to get a bit of warm weather. I put in for the trip, and set out one cold January morning with four others for the sunny south. On our way down we had graphic proof that it is always a good idea to treat any plane with respect if you haven't flown that particular type for some time. Our first stop was Spartanburg, South Carolina. There was a strong wind blowing, slightly at an angle to the main runway. Two of us chose to make our landings on the grassy portion of the field, but the other three pilots landed on the runway, slightly crosswind. Both section leaders dragged their left wings, and we spent a couple of hours on the ground repairing the damage.

The next day we took off for the last leg of the flight. It was still so cold in Atlanta that a chamois face-mask felt good in the open cockpit, but as we approached the Gulf our fur-lined flying suits grew uncomfortably warm. Soon the Florida coastline crept into view, and a short time later we were circling over the Naval Air Station, which had changed so much I hardly recognized it. Station Field had a new asphalt landing mat and new hangars. The old cemetery on the hill and the jungle of scrub pine beyond it had been cleared away, and the space was now occupied by modern new quarters. Everywhere were new buildings, hangars, and bar-racks. The Air Station had really grown up during the two years since I had last seen it.

On the ground the weather was balmy as spring. There were flowers in the gardens and leaves on the trees. The new Bachelor Officers' Quarters where we bunked overnight were the finest I had ever seen, roomy and comfortable. How dif-ferent this was from the old wooden barracks where we had bunked as students!

When we boarded the transport plane that was to take us back to Norfolk after a pleasant weekend, it was with genuine regret that I left Pensacola, and I resolved to return at the first opportunity. Shortly afterward I had my wish. The Navy decided to send thirty-five aviation cadets who had completed two years of active duty with operating squadrons back to Pensacola as flight instructors. I immediately put in my re-quest, and was notified that I had been selected, with orders to report to Pensacola in June.

Other squadron officers received orders to new duty, and once more there was the usual round of farewell parties. Navy life changes each year at the end of the fiscal year in June, when old friends are transferred and new friendships formed. Once more I hated to say goodbye and see them go.

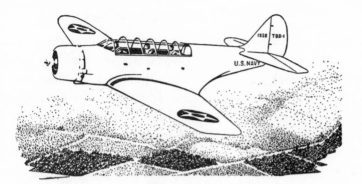

CHAPTER EIGHTEEN

Back to Pensacola

AS SOON AS MY ORDERS TO PENSACOLA AR-
rived, I sent in a request for duty with Squadron Five. For
two years I had been flying single-seaters, and I did not relish
the idea of going back to the sluggish two-seaters in one of
the primary training squadrons. My request was granted, but
I was amazed at the changes in Squadron Five.

Instead of having only seven instructors, the squadron now
had forty-eight, and instead of only single-seaters, there were
three other types of multi-place airplanes in use, including
new TBD-1's, three-place Douglas Torpedo-Bombers with
hydraulically operated folding wings and retractable landing gear, powered by a twin-row 850- H.P. engine; and there
were new NJ-1's, North American Trainers which were the
first low-wing monoplanes the Navy had ever used for student training. There were also a few of the old "flying front-
porches"—the same old TG Torpedo planes I had flown as a
student in Squadron Four, equipped with wheels instead of
the cumbersome floats.

The instrument-flying division was also part of the squadron, with an expanded and improved course which was given in the NJ's. For preliminary instruction in instrument flying there were half a dozen new Link Trainers. In these ingenious machines, students were able to duplicate on the ground most of the maneuvers they could make in an airplane. By means

of a recording pantagraph which traced the theoretical course that the student "flew" under the hood of the Link Trainer, the instructor could follow the course which would have been flown in a real airplane under actual instrument-flying conditions. The student was then shown the tracing made by the pantagraph, which had recorded every movement of the controls that he had made in working out his orientation problems on a radio range, following beam signals exactly like those on the airways.

I was assigned as an instructor in the Flight Division, which included dual instruction in the NJ's, TBD's, and TG's; formation work in the NJ's and F4B-4's; and familiarization, acrobatics, and combat instruction in the F4B-4's. There was a regular course of instruction for instructors, and we were required to check out in each phase of our work before students were assigned to us.

By this time I had logged over eleven hundred hours of flying time—more than some of the instructors who had put me through the course—but I soon found that I was learning to fly all over again. In the fleet squadrons the standards were different; all we had to do was get our planes down safely, and each pilot unconsciously developed his own style of handling his plane. Instruction required standardization, and instructors were expected to equal or exceed the standards which were required of the students. In a single-seater I could skid a turn or correct an overshot approach by sideslipping, but with a student in the cockpit behind me all sloppy flying was out. In order to demonstrate any maneuver properly, smooth flying was imperative. Gradually my own flying improved considerably as I took greater pains to correct it.

The constant variety of the work made it very pleasant. The first hour I might be scheduled to lead a nine-plane formation in slide-over turns or division open-order tactics, while the following hour might be with fighters, marking precision or familiarization landings at Bayou Field, giving primary combat instruction at eight thousand feet over Perdido Bay or marking stunt checks as the students slow-rolled or looped over Corry Field. Then time out for lunch at the Officers' Club rolling poker dice to see who bought the cigars, and back to give an hour of dual instruction in an NJ or TBD. We flew three or four hours a day, and gave lectures or chalk talks the rest of the time. Flying started at seven in the morning during the summer months, and we were off by three in the afternoon, which gave us plenty of time for recreation. The fishing was good as ever. Sharks of the smaller varieties were numerous in Pensacola Bay, and I found that they were more fun on a rod and reel than any fish I had ever caught. The little black-finned sharks, five or six feet long and weighing from fifty to seventy pounds, would walk on their tails when hooked in shallow water, and put up a stiff fight before we could gaff them.

Other cadets reported in shortly afterward, and soon there were nine of us in Squadron Five. Any doubts we had harbored concerning our status were soon dispelled, for we were cordially welcomed and treated like two-stripers. Where we had been flying as wingmen in the fleet, we now flew as division or section leaders in formation maneuvers—invaluable experience that we would have been able to get only after years of duty with an operating squadron. Our students might be officers, cadets, or enlisted men; no distinctions were made. One cadet instructor in the instrument division was assigned two full commanders for students, and both of them commented favorably on his work.

The aerial traffic around Corry Field was more congested than ever, which made it necessary to keep on our toes all the time. Even with all these precautions, I had a few close shaves. One day a student in the front cockpit of an NJ was bringing me in for an approach over the trees south of Corry Field, when the engine suddenly cut out. He tried to stretch his glide and make the field, but I pointed him for an open space between the trees and rolled down full flaps as he made the approach. The plane rolled to a safe stop just short of a sunken road, and I discovered that the student had retarded his mixture control instead of shifting his propeller-pitch lever.

On another occasion a student shifted his gasoline selector valve to the wrong position in a TG, and the big plane's engine quit cold on the take-off when we were about fifty feet in the air. Luckily there was enough field left to set the lumbering giant down safely, for we had an enlisted radio-man in the third cockpit who had a wife and three children.

We had to be particularly careful in our combat instruction. More than one student, in the excitement of his first dog-fight, pulled up so suddenly in front of me that I almost had to do a snap roll to miss him. Some of my closest calls with students, however, were in the big TBD's. One day a student took off for his last solo flight in one of these big torpedo-bombers without locking the wings, which folded on the take-off. The five-ton plane crashed through the roof of the barracks at the edge of the field and the fuel tanks exploded. This fatal accident was followed shortly by a series of others in fleet torpedo squadrons, and although most of these crashes had been due to pilot errors, the students began to think that these big planes were death-traps.

One student brought me in for an approach to Corry Field on a north course, which was the shortest length of the field. As he came in over the trees he forgot to lower his landing flaps. "Put your flaps down," I told him through the gosport speaking tube.

He reached for the hydraulic panel and moved a lever, and I watched the landing gear indicator move to the "up" position as the wheels retracted. "You've got your wheels up," I told him. "Put them down and lower your flaps."

He reached for another lever, and I felt the plane shake

as the hydraulic mechanism tried to fold the wings. Luckily the wing-locking pins held, for we were still a hundred feet in the air. "Go on around and make another approach," I told him.

On his next approach he remembered to lower the flaps, but dove into the field for a hard landing on the wheels. The plane bounced twenty feet in the air. He blasted on full gun and tried to take off over the big administration building dead ahead of us. Grabbing the controls, I chopped the throttle and eased the big ship down to the ground. We rolled to a stop on the lawn in front of the administration building. The student looked back at me, white and shaky.

"You're trying too hard," I told him quietly. "Relax and make me a good one the next time."

He grinned and taxied around for another take-off, and on his next approach he set the plane down in one of the prettiest three-point landings I ever saw. The next hour he soloed without any trouble. His case was typical of dozens I saw. We knew that these students could fly by the time they reached Squadron Five, or they would have been eliminated long before. Most of their trouble was from tenseness or trying too hard, and once they had found out that even the biggest planes were easy to fly, their troubles usually disappeared.

Each instructor in the Flight Division was assigned a class of ten or twelve students, taking them through the syllabus, giving them the lectures on each new phase of the training, and ironing out their difficulties. Thus we grew to know the students pretty well, and some of us were usually invited to their farewell parties after they had completed the course. One class of mine was delayed considerably due to bad weather which kept them grounded for several days during

February. Since this was our slack period, I took this opportunity to go on leave for an automobile trip down to Miami and Key West to do a little fishing.

Just before I left, Jiggs Noble, the squadron's night-flying officer, told me that I was on the night schedule the following week. "As soon as we get a break on the weather," he told me, "I want you to take that class of yours on their night cross-country flight to Atmore."

"Sorry, Jiggs," I answered. "I'm going on leave and won't be back for several weeks."

About ten days later I picked up a newspaper in Miami, and was shocked to read the headlines: "Two Die as Eight Navy Planes Crash In Pensacola Fog." I read on to find that my class had been caught by an unusually heavy fog which rolled in from the Gulf as they returned from the flight on which I had been scheduled to take them. One student who stuck with the instructor landed safely, but two crashed and the rest had to bail out. It was the worst loss that the Pensacola Station had suffered in several years.

Rough weather off Miami had kept me ashore, but that fishing trip was the luckiest one I ever made.

CHAPTER NINETEEN

Air Carnival

WHEN THINGS START TO HAPPEN IN THE AIR, they usually happen pretty fast. If you break the laws of gravitation, you can't go around and have the ticket fixed: you pay the penalty right then and there, according to the degree of your violation. Of course a few variables like altitude, terrain, and luck may mitigate the circumstances, but the chances are that when the emergency comes, you're going to be pressed for time.

The ninth annual National Air Carnival, June 3rd, 1939! Birmingham, Alabama, wealthy metal metropolis of the South, a picture city nestling in a green valley framed by wooded mountains, with Vulcan's statue standing guard on the topmost crest. Real hospitality in the South's finest tradition, with the keys to the city for visiting aviators. That was what we found awaiting us as we left Pensacola, detoured around a few rain squalls, and brought our two sections down on Birmingham's excellent Municipal Airport.

We had three F2F-1 Grumman single-seat fighters and three North American trainers, which were to be on exhibition at the airport, but were not to take an active part in the air carnival, due to an understanding with the Army, who had a National Guard unit on the program. "We'll stake the planes down," our Skipper told us, "and they won't leave the ground until we're ready to take off for home. Those are our orders from the Navy Department. For once we'll be able to see some air races from the spectator's point of view!"

That was all right with the rest of us, but we hadn't counted on Birmingham's hospitality. They deluged us with cocktail parties, banquets, and dances. They swamped us with more invitations than we could have accepted in a month. And everywhere we went, the question was the same: "What kind of a show is the Navy putting on this year?"

After accepting so much hospitality, it was embarrassing to have to reply: "Oh, we're not taking part in the carnival this year. We just came up to watch."

At first this was taken to be a joke, for the newspapers were full of the usual publicity, and the committee had already assigned us a place on the program. But as the first day's events drew to a close, and our planes still sat on the ground, incredulity changed to astonishment, and astonishment to indignation. The committee grew wrathful. *Why* couldn't the Navy participate? After all, it was their Navy! Were we willing? Of course! Did the Army object? Not at all. "Then we'll see about that!" they said. "We'll wire Washington! We'll telephone the Navy Department! We'll call the President!"

The day passed and the night wore on, but still no permission was forthcoming. Then the committee really went on the warpath. Congressmen were kept on the telephone, and senators were aroused from bed. But midnight came, and still our orders were to stay on the ground until we left for home.

Sunday was bright and fair, ideal weather which brought out the largest crowd that had ever attended an air meet. On arising, we hastened to inquire about the day's program, and were not surprised to find that there had been no change in our orders. Since the air show did not begin until one o'clock, we had accepted an invitation to a swimming party. At ten-thirty we were just starting out the door when the Skipper caught us. "We're going to fly!" he told us with a grin. "Our orders are the same as before: we are not to take off until we start home, but we're leaving today instead of tomorrow. However, the committee tells me that the Navy Department has no objections to our circling over the airport a few times, provided that we depart for Pensacola immediately!"

After apologizing to our waiting hosts by telephone, we packed hurriedly and then got together to decide what to do after we took off. Since we had not expected to take part in the Carnival, the only time we had flown together in these particular planes was an hour's loose cruising formation en route to Birmingham. Two hundred thousand people would be watching us perform in a few hours, and they would expect the standards of former Navy demonstrations, which had been presented only after days of painstaking practice.

Our Skipper, Lieutenant Commander Cornwell, wisely chose the simplest course. "Lieutenant Badger's section can do some formation work in the NJ's," he decided, "and we'll go through a dive-bombing routine in the Grummans. No loops, rolls or anything fancy. Without practice, we'd probably botch it."

That was probably the first time that an air show routine was ever rehearsed in a hotel bedroom, but it went off without a hitch, and I doubt if anyone in the crowd could tell the difference. But even at that, I nearly spoiled it, and had a scare that will last me for a long while.

We didn't have much time to get ready, and our planes had been sitting idle on the field for two days. We had only two mechanics with us, who were assisted by airport attendants in servicing our planes. When I arrived at the airport, one of our own squadron mechanics was warming up my plane, and I *took it for granted* that he had done all of the servicing.

Since we had no chocks for the wheels, we had to hold the planes steady with the brakes while we tested the engines. For this reason, I opened my throttle only far enough to see that the engine functioned properly on both magneto switches, then let it idle. If I had opened the throttle as wide as usual for this test, I'd have found out something that would have saved me considerable embarrassment later.

My engine was purring like a kitten. I reached for the rag I always carried in the side of the cockpit and removed a fleck of oil from the windshield. The airstream from the propeller caught the rag and whipped it out of my hand. I started to ask one of the airport attendants to get it for me, but he was busy with another plane, so I *let it go*. Remember that item.

A minute later we were taxying down the concrete apron in front of the biggest crowd I had ever seen. I kept my engine throttled down as much as possible to avoid blowing dust into the crowd as we taxied by, otherwise I'd have found out what I was to learn a short time afterward.

We lined up with all six planes in a right echelon on the ground. The starting bomb exploded overhead, and the Skipper's plane roared off down the runway. As soon as he was rolling, I eased my throttle forward and started to follow. An oily mist fogged my windshield. As I put on full power, more oil sprayed back until I could no longer see through the glass.

By that time I was in the air and past the edge of the field. It was too late to turn back over a crowd like that. With the stick in my left hand, I was cranking the handle that retracted my wheels with my right. The Skipper's plane was on my left. I stuck my head out to keep it in view, and the left side of my goggles got a shot of heavy oil that clouded the glass. Pulling up and over into my position on the Skipper's left, I looked out of the right side, and my goggles were now completely useless. I swept them back off out of the way and squinted out of one eye while I tried to keep in position.

Meanwhile I fully expected that my engine would quit any second. I knew the Skipper would be climbing for altitude, and that my safest bet was to fly on him as long as possible until I could get the oil out of my eyes and see where I was. When I got a glance at the oil pressure gauge, I was relieved to find that it was still up to normal. That made me feel a lot better. At least the engine might not quit right away.

My position was still pretty precarious. I could barely see, and I knew that the three planes behind us were closing rapidly to fly just above me in a tight formation. With one hand on the throttle and the other on the stick, I was busy trying to keep my position at the bottom of a steeply banked turn. I couldn't even wipe the oil out of my eyes until we were squared away on a straight course.

With the back of my shirt sleeve, I finally managed to wipe some of the oil out of my eyes. I cursed my carelessness in taking off without a cloth of some kind to wipe off the windshield. That little piece of greasy rag that I had allowed to blow away would have been worth its weight in pay-checks. Even my handkerchief was out of reach in my hip pocket, underneath the straps of my parachute.

Only the fact that we were still in formation saved me. As long as I could keep the Skipper's plane in sight, I was comparatively safe. But there were four vertical dives awaiting me, two in V formation and two in open attack formation. Before I had time to worry, we were in the first dive. I eased down farther than usual, so that I could keep the Skipper's plane in sight above the top of my clouded windshield. If I had stuck my face out into the slip stream in the vertical dive that followed, the wind blast would have blinded me, for we were really going downhill in a hurry.

To my infinite relief, it worked. As we pulled out of the dive over the center of the field and zoomed back up for another dive, the Skipper looked over and raised his eyebrows questioningly. I nodded to indicate that everything was all right, and he gave the signal for a left echelon. Red crossed over into position behind me, and we swung around over the field for the next dive. This one would be a lot harder.

The Skipper rocked his wings for the attack signal, and whipped his plane over on its back in a quick *reversement*. As soon as he was clear, I started down behind him, knowing that if I ever lost sight of his plane, I was stuck. As my plane

gathered speed in the dive, I eased out to the right far enough
to keep him in view. It may have looked a bit ragged from
the ground, but it saved the day for me. My oil pressure was
still up, and no more oil was flying back in my face.

By using this same procedure, I managed to complete the
remaining dives, and we circled the field to head for home.
We eased out to open cruising formation, and I wiped the oil
and sweat out of my eyes. At last I was able to get at the
handkerchief that should have been within easy reach in my
breast pocket. I wiped off my goggles, and was once more
able to see over the windshield. There was a small rain-squall
dead ahead, and as we plowed through it the driving rain
cleaned most of the oil off the windshield. All my instruments
showed normal readings, so I settled back to relax, vowing
never to be caught short again like that.

There was a good tail-wind, and an hour later we were
circling Corry Field at Pensacola. Back again on the ground,
I found out what had caused all the trouble. In servicing my
plane, someone had over-lubricated the rocker-arms. If I had
opened the throttle wide enough to check the engine properly, I would have discovered this before the take-off. If I had
insisted on having chocks under the wheels, I could have
opened the throttle as wide as I pleased, and if I had taken
the trouble to retrieve the oil rag that I lost, or to have my
handkerchief handy, I could have avoided a bad half-hour
that nearly scared the daylights out of me.

But from now on here's one pilot who isn't going to take off
again in a hurry. You can always change your mind before
you get in the air, but once your wheels are off the ground,
you feel a whole lot more comfortable to know that everything is just right!

CHAPTER TWENTY

Aloha Again

FATE OFTEN PLAYS SUCH STRANGE TRICKS ON us that it is not hard to endow the god of destiny with a personality—a grinning joss who takes a mischievous delight in making mortals eat their own rash statements. Popular opinion likes to picture the average aviator as a man ridden by many superstitions, laden down with good-luck charms and mascots of all kinds, but the opposite is more often the case: men whose longevity depends upon mechanical perfection and accuracy of judgment are inclined to be more practical and hard-headed than others.

Superstition has no place in aviation, yet I must confess that I have a solitary one of my own, which I have learned through sad experience that it is best not to ignore: I'll admit

I'm afraid to tempt fate. Too many times I've made rash statements about the future, vowing that I was all through with some particular place or activity, only to have my own words crammed right back down my throat. After eating bitter crow a few times, I should have learned to hold my tongue about the future. Fate must have overheard my remarks about night flying, for I had never wasted any affection on that branch of our activity since my close call at North Island, the night when I nearly smashed into the cliff at Point Loma. "Night Flying," I had announced, "is the bunk. No self-respecting bird flies at night. Take the owl and the bat, for instance; look at the reputation they have. As far as I am concerned, if I never take off after dark again, it won't break my heart."

I had expected some kind of an unpleasant reaction during night flying after this experience, but was relieved to find nothing more than an increased respect for airplanes in general and night flying in particular. The other pilots might "wring out" their planes with various unnecessary aerobatics during night flights, or go "flat-hatting" around at low altitudes, but not yours truly; from that day on I have confined my night-flying activities strictly to the maneuvers required in the operations orders.

Subsequent experience has not made me any less cautious. Observation of several fatal night-flying accidents convinced me that the danger attending operations after dark are not fully appreciated. With this in mind, I discussed the subject in a magazine article (*Sportsman Pilot*, July 1937), excerpts of which were reprinted in the U. S. Army Air Corps News Letter. While instructing in the instrument-flying division of Squadron Five, I also had an excellent opportunity to study this close relationship between instrument flying and the diffi-culties encountered in contact flying at night.

Then Fate stepped in to take charge of my affairs. One day Lieutenant Paschal, the Chief Flight Instructor, called me in to give me a new assignment. "Starting next month, you'll be the squadron Night-Flying Instructor," he told me. "You'll make out all schedules, give all lectures, and take each student class through the night syllabus."

My other duties included testing the planes which came out of overhaul before assigning them to students, and mak-ing demonstration landings by the light of parachute flares for each incoming class.

"Use the routine test," he continued. "Check the brakes, rigging, tires, and so forth on the ground. In the air, open the throttle wide to see if the oil pressure stays up, then do a snap roll to see if anything is loose. Put the plane on its back for a few seconds to check for fuel or oil leaks, and if she doesn't catch fire, continue the test." He paused and looked at me with a straight face. "Then try a two-turn precision spin each way, to see if the student will be able to get the plane out of any inadvertent spins."

"What if she doesn't come out?" I asked.

He pretended not to hear me. "Then make a vertical dive, not over two hundred knots, with a fairly steep pull-out. Watch the wings for flutter or vibration."

"What if the wings come off?"

"Then the plane is unsafe for students."

"Very simple," I observed. "Now, how about these flare demonstrations?"

"Oh, there's nothing to those," he said easily. "We used to make them in the NJ's, using two flares, but they set the

woods afire, so now we use the single-seaters, with one flare.
As soon as you take off, we turn out all the lights on the field.
You climb to a thousand feet, cut your gun, drop your flare,
and spiral down to a landing by the light of the flare."

"What if I overshoot or undershoot?"

"Now, don't you go making my work harder for me. I'd
have to hunt up a relief for you and break him in all over
again. You'll like this job; you won't have to come to work
until ten the next morning." He grinned at me.

"Here's some more bad news for you," he continued. "The
Navy has decided to kick you upstairs and give you a raise
in pay. You're to report to the commandant's office on the
first of August to receive your ensign's commission."

"Commission!" I exclaimed. "Why, that isn't due until I've
completed my four-year contract, several months from now!"

"I know," he said, "but there has been a change in policy.
From now on, all cadets will be commissioned ensigns as
soon as they leave Squadron Five and get their wings. And
as soon as your four years are up, you are eligible for pro-
motion to lieutenant junior grade."

"Why, that's nearly double our present pay! It's too bad
that we can't stick around for a while longer."

"You can," he grinned. "The Navy is offering you an additional four years of optional active duty. There's no contract
involved this time, and you can request inactive duty at any
time if you have something better lined up on the outside."

"What *could* be better than this?" I asked.

"Oh, I don't know. The airlines will be after you, and there
are a lot of good jobs on the outside for ex-naval aviators.
But it's my own personal belief that the Navy will be able to
use you for a long time to come."

This put an entirely different aspect on the matter. It had been a glorious four-year period, the finest I had ever spent, and I could hardly realize that the time had passed so quickly. The Navy had more than made good everything it had promised me. I had over fifteen hundred hours of flight time behind me—flying experience that couldn't be duplicated on the outside even if I could have spent a private fortune on it. It seemed unfair to shove off and leave a job just when I had reached the peak of my training.

"Don't worry about that angle," was the welcome reassurance. "Even if you do go back to civilian life, you need not leave the Navy. You can go to the nearest Reserve Base and fly all you need to keep your hand in. And if we need you back here, we can always recall you in the event of a national emergency. You're just as valuable in a reserve status as you are on active duty, and we can be training others."

Thus the possibilities before us were almost unlimited. We could continue with a naval career, or return to inactive duty for lucrative jobs on the outside. Many of my group accepted positions with the aircraft companies or with the airlines. The majority requested additional active duty.

What would the future bring? There was war abroad and its attendant rumors. In any event, we were prepared. Whatever happened, most of the old gang would be back together again, flying wing and tail on each other, no matter what the score was.

Sometimes things like that are mighty comforting to know.

Service Identifications

The following system of aircraft model designation is used by the Navy and Marine Corps: on the tail of the airplane is a group of letters and numbers, such as F3F-2. The first letter refers to the type or class of airplane (fighter). The second letter F is the manufacturer's designation (Grumman). The first number indicates that it is the third fighter built by the manufacturer, and the number after the hyphen indicates that this is the second modification. A third modification is the F3F-3. A new model would be an F4F-1. Likewise, a PB2Y-3 is the second model of a patrol-bomber, with a third modification, manufactured by the Consolidated Aircraft Corporation.

Manufacturer's letters and examples follow.

A—Brewster	F2A	Fighter
B—Boeing	F4B-4	Fighter
C—Curtiss	BFC	Bomber-Fighter
D—Douglas	RD	Transport
F—Grumman	F3F-2	Fighter
G—Great Lakes	TG	Torpedo Carrier
J—North American	NJ	Trainer
K—Keystone	NK	Trainer
M—Martin	TM	Torpedo Carrier
N—Naval Aircraft Factory	N2N	Trainer
R—Ford	JR	Utility Plane
S—Sikorsky	XPB2S	Experimental Patrol-Bomber
—Stearman	NS	Trainer
U—Chance-Vought	O2U-2	Observation
Y—Consolidated	NY	Trainer

CLASS DESIGNATIONS

Ambulance	H	Trainer	N
Bomber	B	Transport	R
Experimental	X	Utility	J
Fighter	F	Bomber-Fighter	BF
Observation	O	Scout-Observation	SO
Patrol	P	Patrol-Bomber	PB
Scouting	S	Patrol-Torpedo	PT
Torpedo	T	Torpedo-Bomber	TB

The Marine Corps and the Coast Guard use this same system. The Army and National Guard merely list their successive models, with no manufacturer's designation. Thus an Army P-36 indicates merely that the plane in question is a pursuit ship. The Army uses the following types:

Attack	A	Experimental	Y
Bomber	B	Observation	O
Cargo	C	Pursuit	P

The following key will give the reader some idea of the colors and markings used in Naval and Marine Corps aircraft squadrons:

FIRST DIVISION	SECOND DIVISION
First Section (Red Cowling)	First Section (Black Cowling)
Second Section (White Cowling)	Second Section (Green Cowling)
Third Section (Blue Cowling)	Third Section (Yellow Cowling)

Entire cowling painted, and stripe of same color around fuselage indicates the section leader's plane. The left (No. 2) wingman's plane has the top half of the cowling painted the same color, and the right (No. 3) the bottom half. The chevrons on top of each plane are the same color as the cowlings, and are useful in flying the correct wing position in formation. The top wing is painted yellow in peace time to provide better visibility in the event of a forced landing. The wing insignia (blue circle, white star, red center) is the same on all U. S. service aircraft.

Operating squadrons are now designated according to the aircraft carrier to which they are attached. The carriers are numbered in the order in which they were commissioned, as follows: No. 1, Langley; No. 2, Lexington; No. 3, Saratoga; No. 4, Ranger; No. 5, Yorktown; No. 6, Enterprise; No. 7, Wasp; No. 8, Hornet; etc. Individual planes in a squadron are numbered consecutively: e. g. Scouting Squadron Four, attached to the fourth carrier, the Ranger, has its planes marked 4-S-1, 4-S-2, etc. (pronounced "Four Sail One, Four Sail Two" for clarity over voice radio). The Number Three plane in the third section of a fighting squadron attached to the Enterprise would be 6-F-9 ("Six Fox Nine"), of a bombing squadron 6-B-9 ("Six Baker Nine"), of a torpedo squadron 6-T-9 ("Six Tare Nine"). If a plane were attached to Patrol Squadron Fourteen (no carrier), it would be marked 14-P-9 ("Fourteen Prep Nine"). Thus a pilot from a fighting squadron attached to the Enterprise, calling a pilot from a bombing squadron of the same carrier, might say, "Six Baker Nine from Six Fox Nine: Answer." In time of war, code phrases would be substituted for these numerals to avoid identification.

Up until August 1, 1939, aviation cadets who finished the course at Pensacola were in an officer status, wearing a quarter-inch stripe and a special collar insignia in the form of a small silver fouled anchor. Before graduation they were in a status comparable to that of the midshipman undergraduates of the Naval Academy. Cadets are now commissioned ensigns in the Naval Reserve upon the completion of the course, which now requires approximately six months. They are then transferred to operating squadrons in the fleet.

Many former cadets, including the author, have received commissions in the Regular U. S. Navy, since each year the President is authorized to appoint as commissioned officers of the Regular Navy as many Naval Aviators of the Naval Reserve as he may deem necessary.

This is one of the few times in our Navy's history that naval reserve officers have had the opportunity to qualify for commissions in the line of the Regular Navy on the same basis as graduates of the Naval Academy. Those who do not desire or who are not selected for commissions in the Regular Navy are released from active duty after their period of required service, and thereafter affiliate with the Aeronautic Organization as reserve officers on inactive duty.

Glossary

In the following glossary, some of the aeronautical terms, expressions and colloquialisms used in this book are briefly explained. Many of the definitions are from a pamphlet which is distributed to incoming cadets when they report for instruction at Pensacola. As the pamphlet says, "They should not necessarily be considered proper definitions."

ACE: A student who has had little or no trouble and has acquired a mistaken idea that he is an expert with an airplane.

AILERON: A movable control surface located on the trailing edge of a wing for banking the airplane in turns. Lateral control of the plane is obtained by sidewise movements of the stick, which raises or lowers the ailerons.

APRON: Hard-surfaced area along sea-wall or around a hangar for moving or parking airplanes.

BAILING OUT: Act of jumping from a plane through necessity.

BARREL ROLL: Rapid rotation of a plane on its longitudinal axis through an arc of 360°. Also "Snap

Roll." This aerobatic maneuver, which is merely a horizontal spin, is useful in showing the pilot when to apply corrective controls in recovery from spins or other unusual positions.

BEAM COIL: Removable radio frequency coil installed in certain types of aircraft radios to enable the pilot to tune in on airway directional beam signals.

BLACK-OUT: Temporary loss of vision caused by banking too suddenly at high speeds or pulling out of a dive too abruptly, when excessive centrifugal force drains the blood from the brain. Mild blacking-out is ordinarily harmless; the danger lies in loss of control of the airplane until normal vision returns.

BLIND FLYING: A misnomer applied to what is, or should be, known as instrument flying. Process of flying a plane with the aid of instruments installed in the plane, under such weather conditions that natural aids to flying, such as the horizon, are not available.

CARTWHEEL: A rapid maneuver beginning with a Reverse Control Turn in one direction and ending

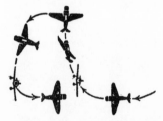

in a similar turn in the opposite direction, in which the nose of the plane is rotated through an arc of 180°. A quick change in heading may thus be effected.

CATERPILLAR CLUB: Any pilot who has been forced to "bail out" of an airplane and whose life has been saved by the caterpillar's silk in the form of a parachute is eligible for this club. Anyone who makes a voluntary jump qualifies for the Ripcord Club if he brings back the parachute ripcord.

CEILING: 1. The height of the lowest cloud layer from the ground.
2. *Absolute* — maximum altitude to which a plane can climb.
3. *Service* — that altitude above which the rate of climb of the plane falls below 100 feet per minute.

CHANDELLE: A climbing turn at high speed, during which the airplane is suddenly turned so as to head in the opposite direction.

CHECK: A flight by a student aviator for the purpose of demonstrating to an accompanying instructor his progress (satisfactory or otherwise) in any phase of the training syllabus.

CHOP: Retard the throttle suddenly to slow down the engine to idling speed. Instructors frequently "chop the throttle" or "cut the gun" to simulate engine failure for emergency landing practice.

CRACK-UP: Any accident with minor damage to the airplane.

CRASH: A serious accident with major damage.

CRATE: Airplane, usually old or slow.

CROSS-COUNTRY: Flights made from one locality to another.

CUT THE GUN: Act of shutting off the gas supply at the carburetor by closing the throttle.

DEAD-STICK LANDING: Landing made with the engine stopped.

DOGFIGHT: Aerial combat between individual airplanes.

"DOWN": Unsatisfactory check flown by a student (*derived from "thumbs down"*).

DROPPED-IN: A hard landing resulting from stalling the plane too high; the opposite of a "hot landing."

ECHELON: Basic formation in which either wingman of a V formation crosses over to a position above and behind the other wingman, so that the leader can drop back to a wing position, or break up the formation by diving out suddenly. (*See page 170.*)

ELEVATOR: A movable control surface located on the tail in a horizontal position just behind the horizontal stabilizer. Also "flipper." Forward or backward movements of the stick raise or lower the elevators, causing the airplane to glide or climb.

FALLING-LEAF: An aerobatic maneuver in which the plane is allowed to stall, and slipped successively to one side and then the

other, the nose being held pointed in approximately the same direction throughout. The resulting motion resembles that of a falling leaf. Useful for determining the spinning characteristics of an airplane.

FIGURE-EIGHT: Maneuver of an airplane in a horizontal plane which causes it to move through an outline of a figure eight. Used in familiarization stages to smooth out airwork.

FIN: See *Vertical Stabilizer.*

FISHTAIL: Swinging of tail from side to side while plane is in normal flying position to lose speed.

FLAT SPIN: Same as tailspin but with nose higher; also, a dizzy state of mind.

FLIPPER: See *Elevator.*

FLIPPER TURN: See *Reverse Control Turn.*

FLYING SPEED: The airspeed at which a plane's wings attain sufficient lift to sustain it in flight.

FORCED LANDING: A landing made necessary because of engine or structural failure.

"G": Gravity. In normal flight, a pilot weighs one "G." In a steeply banked turn or a steep pull-out from a dive, centrifugal force will push him down in the cockpit with a force of several times his own weight, or several "G's." In a five-G pull-out, he will probably "black out" temporarily until normal flight is resumed.

GLIDE: Descent of plane with normal forward motion resulting from pull of gravity only.

GROUND LOOP: Uncontrolled swerving of plane from a straight course while rolling over the ground after landing.

HALF ROLL: The first or last half of a slow roll. Useful for entering a dive or recovering from unusual positions.

HORIZONTAL STABILIZER: A tail surface which is secured in a horizontal position, just ahead of the elevators, and usually adjustable in flight from the pilot's cockpit.

HORIZONTAL BOMBING: Bombing from level flight, which is the technique used by patrol planes and other high-altitude bombers, as opposed to dive bombing, in which the bomb is aimed by pointing the airplane at the target in a steep dive.

HOT LANDING: Landing made with the plane not in a fully stalled attitude, usually with excess speed.

IMMELMAN TURN: A 180° turn

made by half a loop followed by a half roll.

JENNIE: Wartime training plane, coined from the manufacturer's designation JN.

KNOTS: Nautical miles per hour. A knot is approximately one and one-sixth land miles per hour. 100 knots equals 116 m.p.h.; 300 knots, 348 m.p.h.; etc. All Navy air-speed indicators are calibrated in knots, since most of their flight operations are conducted from ships at sea, which requires celestial navigation to coordinate their relative movements.

LINE: Basic formation in which planes are lined up left or right on the leader, wing tip to wing tip. (*See page 81.*)

LOOP: A complete turn made in the vertical plane. This is one of the

first primary aerobatic maneuvers that the student learns, and it helps him to become accustomed to unusual positions.

OPEN OUT: Increase distance between planes in formation.

OVERSHOOT: To land beyond, (or miss landing completely) a desired landing point, due to miscalculation, excessive speed, etc.

PEEL OFF: To dive out from the bottom of an echelon formation.

POUR THE SOUP: Act of giving more gas to the engine by opening the throttle.

POWER DIVE: A dive made with the engine furnishing power.

PROP: Propeller.

PYLON: A three or four-sided structure built up to a point, used for a ground marker.

RADIO BEAM: Directional radio signals on Civil Aeronautics Authority airways which are focused along a narrow path or beam. Pilots tuning in on these signals are able to determine their position with relation to the station from which the signals emanate.

RANKING:

Navy & Coast Guard	Army & Marine Corps
Ensign	2nd Lieutenant
Lt. (junior grade)	1st Lieutenant
Lieutenant	Captain
Lieutenant Commander	Major
Commander	Lieutenant Colonel
Captain	Colonel
Rear Admiral	Brigadier General
Vice Admiral	Major General
Admiral	General

RAT RACE: Tail-chasing. Open-order squadron maneuvers, usually through air made turbulent by the slip streams of planes ahead.

RENDEZVOUS: To join up individual planes in a section, or sections in a division. A designated area where a formation can join up.

RESERVE BASE: The Navy has sixteen naval reserve aviation bases, located at Washington, Philadelphia, Kansas City, Seattle, Oakland, St. Louis, Minneapolis, Detroit, Brooklyn, Miami, Boston, Chicago, Long Beach, Dallas, New Orleans, and Atlanta. Complete information can be had by writing to any of these bases.

REVERSE CONTROL TURN: A turn in which the bank exceeds 45°, at which point the controlling

functions of the elevator and rudder are largely interchanged. Also called "flipper" turns (flipper = elevator) because with more than 45° bank the turning force is derived from the flipper.

ROLL ON TOP: A loop at high speed, with a snap roll at the top of the loop. Purely an acrobatic maneuver.

SHOOTING SMALL FIELDS: Approaching and sometimes landing a plane in small-sized fields.

SHOOTING THE CIRCLE: Attempting to land in an area bounded by a circle with a diameter of 100′ marked out in certain practice fields, without the aid of the engine. The engine is throttled down to idling speed at a designated altitude and position with respect to the wind, and the plane so maneuvered to land inside the circle.

SKIDDING: Sidewise motion of a plane in the line of flight caused by use of excessive rudder control.

SKIPPER: The commanding officer of a Naval Station, base, ship, or squadron, who is usually addressed by the personnel under his command as "Captain," no matter what his rank.

SLIPPING: Sidewise motion of a plane away from the line of flight when engine power is being deliv-

ered. Any sidewise motion when gliding caused by excessive bank. Slipping may be intentional or not; it may be used, for example, to lose altitude without gaining speed, in approaching for a landing.

SLIP STREAM: The turbulent or disturbed air in the wake of an airplane. Gusty air will often cause a plane to stall at a flying speed above its normal stalling speed, and violent slip streams can throw a plane into an inadvertent spin.

SLOW ROLL: Slow rotation of a

plane on its longitudinal axis through an arc of 360°.

SNAP ROLL: See *Barrel Roll*.

SPIN IN: To fail to recover from a spin before the plane strikes the ground or water. From any considerable altitude, this would normally result in complete demolition of the airplane.

SPLIT-S TURN: A turn made by pulling the nose of a plane up into a steep climb until it reaches the stalled position. Rudder is then applied, which puts the airplane in an inverted position. Recovery is effected by diving out, which leaves the plane headed in the opposite direction — a quick way to reverse course.

SQUADRON: Operating unit in the fleet. Carrier squadrons usually consist of eighteen planes, in two nine-plane divisions of three sections each.

STALL:

1. The air-speed at which an air-

plane's wings cease to have lifting power to sustain it.

2. A *power stall* is a power-on approach in which the airplane is allowed to settle slowly at an air-speed just above the stalling point.

3. A *whip stall* is a stall from a vertical climb, from which the airplane's nose whips violently forward.

4. A *hammerhead stall* is a stall from a vertical climb, from

which the airplane falls off on one wing in a hammer-like motion.

TAIL SPIN: Spinning motion an air-

plane assumes when falling out of control after losing flying speed.

TERMINAL VELOCITY: The maximum speed which a plane can reach in a vertical dive.

THREE-POINT LANDING: A landing which is made with the two wheels and the tail wheel hitting the ground simultaneously.

UNDERSHOOT: To come in for a landing short of the mark desired.

"UP": A successful squadron flight check made by a student (derived from "thumbs up").

V: Basic formation in the shape of the letter V, copied from the cruising formations of wild geese. *(See page 74.)*

VERTICAL STABILIZER: A vertical airfoil, forward of the rudder, usually adjustable through a small arc, whose function is to give a plane directional stability. Also called vertical fin.

WASH-OUT: Complete wreck.

WING-OVER: A maneuver in which a change of direction of 180° is effected, beginning with a radi-

cally nose-high turn flown practically to a stall 90° from the original heading, with recovery 180° from the original heading. Useful for reversing course quickly.

ZOOM: A dive followed by a pull-up of the plane to its original position, with or without power. Used to signal while in formation, to call attention, or just to show off.

About the Author

Robert A. Winston was born in Washington, Indiana, in 1907 and graduated from Indiana University. He worked for *The New York Times* and *The New York News* for five years before starting flight training with the navy in 1935. He flew in fighting squadrons on both coasts and as an instructor at Pensacola, and he wrote about his initial aviation training in *Dive Bomber,* published in 1939 when Winston held the rank of lieutenant. In his second book, *Aces Wild,* he chronicled his experiences in Europe during 1939–40 as a test pilot accompanying a consignment of fighters destined for Finland. Back on active duty in the United States, he served as a flight instructor, then in the public relations office in Washington, D.C. After the attack on Pearl Harbor he was assigned to combat duty in the Pacific, which he recounts in *Fighting Squadron,* published in 1946 when Winston was a commander. At the end of the war he was serving on Admiral Nimitz's staff on Guam. From there he moved to Stockholm, where he served as the naval air attaché.

The **Naval Institute Press** is the book-publishing arm of the U.S. Naval Institute, a private, nonprofit professional society for members of the sea services and civilians who share an interest in naval and maritime affairs. Established in 1873 at the U.S. Naval Academy in Annapolis, Maryland, where its offices remain today, the Naval Institute has more than 100,000 members worldwide.

Members of the Naval Institute receive the influential monthly magazine *Proceedings* and discounts on fine nautical prints, ship and aircraft photos, and subscriptions to the quarterly *Naval History* magazine. They also have access to the transcripts of the Institute's Oral History Program and get discounted admission to any of the Institute-sponsored seminars regularly offered around the country.

The Naval Institute's book-publishing program, begun in 1898 with basic guides to naval practices, has broadened its scope in recent years to include books of more general interest. Now the Naval Institute Press publishes more than forty new titles each year, ranging from how-to books on boating and navigation to battle histories, biographies, ship and aircraft guides, and novels. Institute members receive discounts on the Press's more than 375 books.

Full-time students are eligible for special half-price membership rates. Life memberships are also available.

For a free catalog describing the Naval Institute Press books currently available, and for further information about U.S. Naval Institute membership, please write to:

Membership & Communications Department
U.S. Naval Institute
Annapolis, Maryland 21402

Or call, toll-free, (800) 233-USNI. In Maryland, call (301) 224-3378.

THE NAVAL INSTITUTE PRESS

DIVE BOMBER
Learning to Fly the Navy's Fighting Planes

Set in Century Schoolbook

Printed on 55-lb. Warren Sebago, cream-white
and bound in Holliston Roxite A
by R.R. Donnelley & Sons Company
Harrisonburg, Virginia